Questions of Judgment

Questions of Judgment

Determining What's Right

F. H. Low-Beer

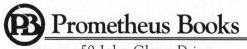 Prometheus Books

59 John Glenn Drive
Amherst, NewYork 14228-2197

Published 1995 by Prometheus Books

99 98 97 96 95   5 4 3 2 1

Library of Congress Cataloging-in-Publication Data

Low-Beer, F. H. (Frank H.)
    Questions of judgment: determining what's right / F. H. Low-Beer.
        p.   cm.
    Includes bibliographical references and index.
    ISBN 0-87975-960-7
    1. Judgment (Ethics) 2. Decision-making. 3. Reasoning.
I. Title.
BJ1408.5.L68   1995
153.4'6—dc20   95-8726
                                                                    CIP

Printed in the United States of America on acid free paper.

For my mother
who knew that what is most
important is to know what is

Contents

8   Contents

Preface

As a working lawyer I became aware from a wide practice that success in the professions depends on something not reducible to knowledge, intelligence, or diligence. Stints in politics and responsibility for investment management confirmed this observation. It became clear that failure even more than success is attributable to what is called the exercise of judgment. I asked whether this phrase, pervasive in diverse fields, refers to the same mental process. What sort of activity is this exercise? And what is meant by calling something "a question of judgment"? When are issues questions of judgment, and when are they not? Is the phrase meant to distinguish questions of preference or taste from fact? What are the features of judgment generally? Is the judgmental function at work surreptitiously? Is it tangled with character? Can it be taught?

Surprisingly, although some titles promised much, no comprehensive study of judgment was to be found. I started to make notes. So this book had its beginning. The subject got away from me. It led to fields that refused to be circumscribed and were entered with trepidation. Yet they deserved notice. For one purpose was to bring the ubiquity of judgment to the fore and see whether its instances could be brought under one roof. To bring home the reach of the concept, I have not shied from juxtaposing

9

theory with what may appear out of the way. Hence there is a cumbersome breadth, the depth to be supplied by others. While there are occasional lapses, I draw back from some of the deeper theoretical implications of the general notion of judgment to explore the more clearly bounded aspect of judgment as exercise that directly brings in the notions of importance and appropriateness. Still, to situate that aspect in its setting I touch on neighboring areas where judgment is not clearly distinguishable from other aspects of thought. Because the discussion crisscrosses the subject from many sides, its texture is perforce uneven. There was also the thorny issue of the appropriate pitch for the inquiry, never quite resolved. One attempt was to return notes as leavening to the bottom of the page where the reader could follow side paths to other levels. Judgments all.

Because of the varied background from which the book arose, the acknowledgments of advice and help usually found in a preface are largely absent. Yet there are friends to whom thanks are due. When some years ago I asked Donald Davidson what work had been done on the exercise of judgment, he pointed me without hesitation to Aristotle and stopped. Before and since, Davidson's thought has been the jumping off point for my own ideas. I have profited greatly from his comments on a draft midway through. I owe much to George Woodcock, whose rare appreciation for what I was attempting sustained the effort till his death as the book went to press. I'm indebted in a quite special sense to my children for leads, talk, and encouragement. I'm also grateful to my long-time partners for the accumulated collegial experience, of which much said here is a by-product. Finally, I thank Tirthankar Bose for deft editorial computer assistance and Maud Smith for patient stenography in the early stages.

Introduction

Since the Pre-Socratic philosophers, the high ground of Western thought has been occupied by the quest for knowledge and certainty. Some dominant peaks are easy to identify: Plato, Aristotle, Aquinas, Bacon, Descartes, Spinoza, Leibniz, Hume, Kant. Along the way theology broke off as a spur; later the chain divided into two ranges, philosophy and natural science.

From one of the early peaks, Aristotle, a slight stream ran down to the valley where it meandered through the centuries, occasionally reduced to a trickle but here and there broadening into a quiet reach where it carried the main message of human thought. The way stations on this stream were thinkers like Marcus Aurelius, Erasmus, Montaigne, Voltaire, Emerson, and Dewey. Up on the main range, knowledge, the high aim of Western thought, strove for a true and certain picture of reality through reason or faith, and later, perception and experience. The picture in the mind was to correspond to the world one-to-one. The thinkers in the valley, because they were not concerned directly with knowledge and reality but primarily with human conduct, saw no need to dwell on certainty. Reason itself was not sufficient to attain the good life they celebrated. Another more complex and elusive quality of mind not always explicitly recognized was at stake. What judgment worked on did not fit easily into categories of true and false, sidestepping the thirst for certainty that drove Western thought. Because these thinkers were not logicians, metaphysicians, or scientists, their occasional remarks on judgment were relegated to the periphery.

It is not my aim to trace that slight stream from its source but to tap it as it emerges into the present day. A brief overview will show that writers, in the scattered pages devoted to it, thought of judgment variously as a stand-in for knowledge, as particular assertion, as the outcome of inquiry, and as the process of reaching such outcome. But the treatment has been cursory and spotty. My attempt is to get clear on what it is to judge and its intellectual and social significance. What it is to judge in turn requires consideration of both how the *use* of "judge" in the language differs from "decide," "believe," "assert," "know," and other terms referring to goings-on in the mind, and the wider consideration of the *judgmental function,* whether it is reflected in language or not. Is judgment a unitary concept? What is a question of judgment and what is not? The concern will be primarily with judgment as process, what we call the *exercise* of judgment, a departure from the traditional treatment that focuses only on the product. While they may first leap to mind, what are called value judgments will not be my main concern, although they are implicated. What goes into determining *what's right* generically is at issue, not the special case of determining the morally right decision.

I will suggest that it is useful to consider judgment as a definable second-order cognitive process yet coequal in importance to the primary ones of intelligence and imagination. I start by noting how deeply embedded judgment is in our everyday lives, how we depend on it at every turn. Its critical role in our social institutions and practices will become apparent. By examining those where judgment is foundational—the law, the professions, politics, commerce—we may find confirmation of its essential elements. Are these elements sufficiently similar to justify using the expression over the whole domain? Is there a common decision-making process at a deep level that underlies disparate fields not usually linked? To what extent do questions of judgment underlie not only practice but belief? To attempt an answer one must be rash enough to mix reflections on the everyday with the theoretical, and to cross closely guarded interdisciplinary lines.

In a substantial way the domain discussed as judgment overlaps what has traditionally been treated under the heading Practical Reasoning, concerned with deliberations relating to conduct. I argue that recognizing the centrality of the judgmental function is a more comprehensive paradigm than the stark want-belief model. Judgment appears as the inner regulatory device, the guardian at the gate of belief which may or may not lead to action. To the extent our beliefs are monitored, the distinction disappears between practical and other sorts of deliberation. A pristine view of reasoning sees it as links in the judgmental process. While there is a sense in which judgment can be subsumed under rationality, important distinctions are masked by doing so. Judgment is both prior to, and in another sense post, what is usually thought of as rationality, which raises issues that have been missed in recent writing on the objectivity of reasons and values. The neighboring area that also needs distinguishing is interpretation.

To label an issue a question of judgment is a cognitive put-down. The implication is that such issues are outcasts from knowledge, that worthwhile issues deserve something better than judgment. I attempt to right the put-down first by stressing that far more issues than we are prone to believe turn on judgment, and second by arguing that judgment is critical to cognition itself. As the concept of knowledge as a mirror of reality clouds, the exercise of judgment comes to the fore as a self-contained cognitive process, with an autonomous status not traditionally acknowledged. Throughout, judgment is identified as the key to determining what is right in the particular circumstance. Accepting its central place leads to a look at the extent to which judgment can be learned, its reciprocal relationship to character, and how its exercise defines us.

I

A Glance Up the Valley

The judgment of man is fallible.
—Ovid *Fasti* v. c.5

If you judge, investigate. (Si judicas, cognosce.)
—Seneca *Medea* c.60

All general judgments are loose and imperfect.
—Michel de Montaigne, *Essays,* III (1588)[1]

It is remarkable that the thinker who has dealt most extensively with the judgmental function in the history of ideas appears close to its beginning. We plunge into the thick with Aristotle in the opening paragraphs of the *Nicomachean Ethics* and at once detect how important judgment is to his epistemic and moral universe. In the following passage on politics, judgment is already in the wings:

---

1. Quotations at the beginning of chapters are from H. L. Mencken, *A New Dictionary of Quotations* (New York: Alfred A. Knopf, 1942).

Our account of this science will be adequate if it achieves such clarity as the subject-matter allows; for the same degree of precision is not to be expected in all discussions, any more than in all the products of handicraft. Instances of morally fine and just conduct—which is what politics investigates—involve so much difference and variety that they are widely believed to be such only by convention and not by nature. Instances of goods involve a similar kind of variety, for the reason that they often have hurtful consequences. People have been destroyed before now by their money, and others by their courage. Therefore in discussing subjects, and arguing from evidence, conditioned in this way, we must be satisfied with a broad outline of the truth; that is, in arguing about what is for the most part so from premises which are for the most part true we must be content to draw conclusions that are similarly qualified. The same procedure, then, should be observed in receiving our several types of statement; *for it is a mark of the trained mind never to expect more precision in the treatment of any subject than the nature of that subject permits; for demanding logical demonstrations from a teacher of rhetoric is clearly about as reasonable as accepting mere plausibility from a mathematician.* [Emphasis mine]

(Ethics I.iii.1094b)

We are drawn up short by the sheer modernity of the directness and tone of this passage which contrasts so starkly with what went before. We sense here Aristotle's commitment to the everyday world around him. And its silent tribute to the test of *appropriateness* would have been quite foreign to the absoluteness of Plato.[2]

---

2. Donald Davidson in conversation has questioned the severity of "quite foreign," pointing to the *Philebus*. Plato there concludes that wisdom (the good) must partake of some degree of pleasure, and likewise of reason. The mixture of the two depends on measure and proportion. Indeed, the possession of measure and proportion is there accorded the first rank. But for all that, there is for Plato an absoluteness and fixity about this very mixture and degree, a characteristic frozen state in which measure, proportion, and degree are pre-determined and do not depend on the continuous exercise of human judgment. Appropriateness touches something beyond measure and proportion.

The appeal to appropriateness we find in Aristotle cannot be determined without the exercise of judgment. It is not surprising that he celebrates judgment in regard to the *moral* virtues of tact, prudence, and the mean. What is remarkable is that for Aristotle judgment in the sense of *exercise* is an *intellectual* virtue and has a part to play in cognition.

Aristotle employs different terms to convey different aspects of what we understand as judgment.[3] Judgment as opinion he rejects as a way to truth, but judgment as prudence (*phronesis*) he praises. One of the features of prudence is that it "involves knowledge of particular facts, which become known from experience" (*Ethics* VI.viii. 1141b). He goes on to apply this to politics:

> Political science and prudence are the same state of mind but their essence is not the same. Prudence concerning the State has two aspects: one, which is controlling and directive, is legislative science; the other, which deals with particular circumstances, bears the name that properly belongs to both, viz., political science. This latter is practical and deliberative; for an enactment is a thing that can be done, and the last step in a deliberative process.
>
> (*Ethics* VI.viii.1141b)

What Aristotle means is that the last step in the analysis, that is, making the judgment, becomes the first in the ensuing course of action. On this he is, as we will see, close to Dewey. He sees the connection between judgment and choice. "Now the origin of action (the efficient not the final cause) is choice" (*Ethics,* VI. ii.1139b).

About prudence, also translatable as common sense and practical wisdom, he says,

> We may grasp the nature of prudence if we consider what sort of people we call prudent. . . . [W]e call people prudent in particular respects when they have calculated successfully with a

---

3. In the following pages "judgment," "appropriateness," and "importance" appear repeatedly. For the sake of simplicity, the functions of these terms to refer variously to concepts, aspects of mental process, or criteria will not always be spelled out and will be determined by the context.

view to some serious end (outside the sphere of art); so that in
general also the man who is capable of deliberation will be prudent—it is a true state, reasoned, and capable of action with
regard to things that are good or bad for man. . . . [H]e ought
to make every choice as a means to that end and perform every
act on account of it. . . . Thus prudence must be a true state reasoned and capable of action in the sphere of human goods.

(Ethics VI.v.1140a)

A bit further on Aristotle says with respect to judgment
(*gnome*) and consideration:

What is called judgment in virtue of which we say that people
are considerate and have sympathetic judgment is the faculty
of judging correctly what is equitable. An indication of this is
the common view that the equitable man is especially sympathetic in his judgments and that it is equitable to judge sympa-
thetically in circumstances and sympathetic judgment is a correct judgment that decides what is equitable; a correct judgment being one that arrives at the truth.
    All these states of mind naturally tend to coalesce, because
we attribute judgment, understanding, prudence, and intelligence to the same persons saying indifferently that they now
have a mature judgment and intelligence, and that they are prudent and understanding. For all these faculties are concerned
with ultimate or particular things and to be an understanding and
considerate or sympathetic person consists in being able to judge
about those things about which the prudent man is concerned;—
that is why these states are considered to be natural gifts, whereas no one is thought to be endowed by nature with wisdom,
although he may have judgment, understanding, and intuition.

(Ethics VI.xi.1143a)

There is still another ingredient in Aristotle's concept of judgment—resourcefulness or deliberation (*euboulia*):[4]

---

4. I am indebted to a lucid account by David Wiggins (1975) of Aristotle's
concept of deliberation and practical reasoning, in which he sees Aristotle as
maintaining that no general rules can be laid down for practical reasoning, an
issue that is taken up here from different directions in later chapters.

Well, it [deliberation] is not knowledge; for people do not enquire about things that they know, and resourcefulness is a kind of deliberation, and a person who is deliberating inquires and calculates. But to inquire is not the same as to deliberate; because deliberation is a sort of inquiry. What is more, it is not ability to conjecture either; because this is a rapid thing independent of reasoning, whereas deliberation goes on for some time.

(*Ethics* VI.ix.1142a)

In these passages we see how central and pervasive the exercise of judgment is to Aristotle's conception of our mental and moral life. While we need not follow Aristotle in concluding so readily that prudence and judgment are natural gifts or in bracketing judgment with intelligence and understanding, we can allow his concepts of *gnome, phronesis,* and *euboulia* to coalesce into our concept of judgment. Note that while he classifies these concepts as intellectual rather than moral virtues, the qualities of judgment and common sense heavily tinge his moral outlook.

Finally, running through the entire discussion of judgment is its critical connection with the particular:

Again, prudence is not concerned with universals only; it must also take cognizance of particulars, because it is concerned with conduct, and conduct has its sphere in particular circumstances.

(*Ethics* VI.vii.1141b)

For the scientific truth is demonstrable, whereas art and prudence are only concerned with the variable.

(*Ethics* VI.vi.1140b)

It is obvious that prudence is not scientific knowledge, because it apprehends the last step—prudence apprehends the ultimate particular, which cannot be apprehended by scientific knowledge but only by perception—not that of objects peculiar to one sense, but the sort by which we perceive that the ultimate figure is a triangle.

(*Ethics* VI.viii.1142a)

These passages from the *Ethics* have been cited not to give a comprehensive account of Aristotle's position, but rather to take advantage of a fortuitous review at the beginning of our intellectual history of related concepts that have stimulated the present inquiry. Whatever disagreement we might have with the minute distinctions Aristotle makes between these concepts variously translated as practical reasoning, practical wisdom, prudence, consideration, resourcefulness, and deliberation, we can agree that this large family, which may be seen as aspects of the exercise of judgment, has not received such devoted attention since.

In Roman times, while there was little concern with the part that judgment plays in our intellectual processes, judgment and discretion were celebrated as moral virtues and as guides to successful conduct. One thinks of the Stoics, Cicero, the rhetoricians, and Marcus Aurelius, who counseled reason and moderation. There was talk of a *sensus communis* which partook of a political sense of community as well as common sense.

In the fifteenth and sixteenth centuries one thinks of Erasmus. How can one distinguish a flatterer from a true counselor? How can one profit even from an enemy? And there are the well-known tips on conduct by Machiavelli and Castiglione. These how-to books in exercising judgment were intended to lead to the ideal of the Renaissance man as *uomo universale.* Practical humdrum stuff perhaps, but significant for its emphasis on process.

Above all, at the end of this period one thinks of Montaigne, who was preoccupied with judgment as central to the widest range of our everyday concerns. Scanning the table of contents of his *Essays* gives a feel for the mental qualities to which Montaigne gave weight: "On Moderation," "Goods and Evils Depend Upon Opinion," "Of the Inequality Amongst Us," "Of Custom," "That We Should Not Easily Change a Law Received," "On Measuring Truth and Error," "That a Man Is to Judge Soberly of Divine Ordinances." In an essay titled "Of the Uncertainty of Our Judgment" Montaigne deals with countless instances of good and bad judgment on the part of military commanders. He recites various arguments pro and con that Francis I considered in determining to meet the invading Emperor

Charles V in the Provence rather than marching out to meet him in Italy. By considering similar decisions made by Hannibal (that correct strategy in one instance is the wrong strategy in another) Montaigne concludes skeptically:

> By which examples and divers others we are wont to conclude, and with some reason, that events, especially in war, do for the most part depend upon fortune who will not be governed by, nor submit unto human prudence. According to the poet— "Prudence deceitful and uncertain is, ill counsels sometimes hit where good ones miss."—But if things hit right it should seem that our counsels and deliberations depend as much upon fortune as anything else we do, and that she engages our very reason in arguments in her uncertainty and confusion.
>
> (Montaigne 1743, v.1, 345)

In "Of Democritus and Heraclitus" Montaigne comes closer to a direct approach to judgment:

> That judgment is a utensil proper for all subjects and will have an oar in everything which is the reason that in these essays I take hold of all occasions; where though it happened to be a subject I do not very well understand, I try however sounding it at a distance and finding it too deep for my stature I keep me on the firm shore; in this knowledge that a man can proceed no further is one effect of its virtue even in the most inconsidering sort of men.
>
> (Montaigne 1743, v.1., 345)

In an essay on "Cripples" Montaigne begins by noting that the year had been made ten days shorter in France and continues:

> What a fine condition are we in to keep records of things passed! I was just now ruminating as I often do upon this what a free and roving thing human judgment is.
>
> (Montaigne 1743, v.1., 290)

By contrast to the humanism of the preceding century, the seventeenth century marked a sharp swing toward a new scholas-

ticism—rigorous logic and the celebration of knowledge and certainty. The black-and-white mapping of mind focused on fields
that were served by that approach: metaphysics, epistemology,
astronomy, physics, mathematics. The religious dogmatism of
the time was mirrored by a corresponding intellectual absolutism
in the works of Descartes, Pascal, Spinoza, Leibniz, and Newton.
The preoccupation with reason, certainty, and precision left no
place for such gray and cloudy concepts as judgment, except as
clear affirmation.[5]

The eighteenth century saw a softening of this one-dimensional approach to cognition. The English empiricists did not
simply substitute sensation for reason as a path to truth. In a higher sense they expanded sensation into experience which, as Aristotle saw, was closely linked to judgment. That softening may be
traced back one century to Hobbes who saw judgment primarily
as discernment, discrimination, and as discretion when applied to
matters of daily living. Understanding the discrete elements of a
problem constituted good judgment (*Leviathan,* chapter 8). There
is something of Hobbes's concept of judgment in Locke, for
whom judgment is a kind of assertion based on best estimate:

> The understanding faculties being given to man, not barely for
> speculation, but also for the conduct of his life, man would be
> at a great loss if he had nothing to direct him but what has the
> certainty of true knowledge. For that being very short and
> scanty, as we have seen, he would be often utterly in the dark,
> and in most of the actions of his life perfectly at a stand, had
> he nothing to guide him in the absence of clear and certain
> *knowledge.* He that will not eat till he has demonstration that it
> will nourish him, he that will not stir till he infallibly knows the
> business he goes about will succeed, will have little else to do

---

5. "According to Descartes, judgement involves both the understanding and the will. His view is that the understanding is necessary to 'perceive' a proposition—by 'perceive' he apparently means 'entertain'—but
'the will is absolutely essential for our giving assent to what we have in
some manner perceived.' . . . Unlike Descartes, Spinoza holds that an idea
and a volition, or the faculties of the intellect and the will are one and the
same, so that for Spinoza an idea is a judgement" (Parkinson 1954, 93–94).

but sit still and perish. . . . The faculty which God has given man to supply the want of clear and certain knowledge, in cases where that cannot be had, is *judgment*: whereby the mind takes its *ideas* to agree or disagree or, which is the same, any proposition to be true or false, without perceiving a demonstrative evidence in the proofs. The mind sometimes exercising this *judgment* out of necessity where demonstrative proofs and certain knowledge are not to be had and sometimes out of laziness, unskillfulness, or haste, even where demonstrative and certain proofs are to be had. . . . This faculty of mind, when it is exercised immediately about things, is called *judgment*; . . . Thus the mind has two faculties conversant about truth and falsehood: First, *knowledge,* whereby it certainly perceives and is undoubtedly satisfied of the agreement or disagreement of any ideas. Secondly, *judgment,* which is the putting ideas together or separating them from one another in the mind, when their certain agreement or disagreement is not perceived but presumed to be so; which is, as the work imports, taken to be so before it certainly appears. And if it so unites or separates them as in reality things are, it is *right judgment*. . . . As demonstration is the showing the agreement or disagreement of two ideas by the intervention of one or more proofs which have a constant, immutable, and visible connexion one with another, so *probability* is nothing but the appearance of such an agreement or disagreement by the intervention of proofs whose connexion is not constant and immutable, or at least is not perceived to be so, but is or appears for the most part to be so, and is enough to induce the mind to *judge* the proposition to be true or false, rather than the contrary.

(Locke 1964, 247)

Berkeley follows Locke in applying the fallibility of judgment to the certainty of perception. Berkeley places judgment in the "judicial department" of the mind as an essential element of knowledge. Significantly, Berkeley points to common sense as an underlying current running through British philosophy, to which he felt obliged to appeal to justify his more extravagant conclusions. Reason mellowed to reasonableness.

Common sense is close to the surface in Hume's writing. He

has much to say on what has traditionally been called "practical reasoning," as discussed later under that heading. In a footnote Hume dismissed the "vulgar division" between conception, *judgment,* and reasoning, and maintains that in effect the significant act of the mind "never yet explained by any philosopher" is the joining of an idea with the confidence of its truth, that is, assertion. His diplomatic example given of such a judgment: "God is" (Hume 1975, 96). Hume's emphasis on experience as a foundation of knowledge coupled with respect for common sense (he is thought of as leader of the Scottish school of common-sense philosophers) implies a recognition of judgment as central to cognition (Ayer 1980).

The ideal of the Renaissance man cropped up in a new guise in the eighteenth-century Enlightenment as the well-rounded gentleman who diluted the rationalism filtered from the preceding century with the detached but worldly common sense of Montaigne. There was in the air in England and France, as previously in Rome, a preoccupation (perhaps not untypical of the establishments of prosperous imperial societies) with the subtleties of social relations. The result was the application of the judgmental qualities of discretion, moderation, and reasonableness not only to personal conduct but to political and social concerns, as seen in Burke and Voltaire. In Italy we have Giambattista Vico reaching back to the Roman concept of a *sensus communis* and applying it to his historicism (Gadamer 1992, 19).

Toward the end of the eighteenth century, in a quite different way, we find Kant coming to judgment from the undiluted rationalist tradition. Since Aristotle, Kant's was the first sustained treatment of the concept, deeply embedded in his thought. His head-on approach is not from a concern with human conduct but from his quest to justify confidence in every intellectual endeavor. He appeals to the expression *Urteil* in two different ways. The first is as an assertion, a claim to truth. For example, in the introduction to the *Critique of Pure Reason,* Kant says, "All mathematical judgments are synthetic." Why *judgments*? Why did he not go straight to *assertions* or other neutral claims to knowledge? Perhaps Kant is driven to this odd formulation because he accepts Plato's view that a true judgment is knowledge. His famous question "How are synthetic judgments a priori possible?" is also couched in the language of judgment. Judgment is here used in a quite different sense from Locke's use as a *stand-in* for knowledge.[6]

Kant's other apparently different use of judgment runs through the *Critique of Judgment* (*Kritik Der Urteilskraft*) written in the closing years of his working life. The work is in two parts, *The Critique of Aesthetic Judgment* and *The Critique of Teleological Judgment*. Kant saw aesthetic judgment as an assertion justifiable by example only. How judgment in this sense was related to knowledge and cognition is not at all clear. Consider the following extracts from the preface and introduction to the *Critique of Judgment*:

> But now comes judgment which in the order of our cognitive faculties forms a middle term between understanding and reason—A critique of pure reason, i.e. of our faculty of judging on a priori principles, would be incomplete if the critical examination of judgment, which is a faculty of knowledge, and as such lays claim to independent principles, were not dealt with separately.
>
> (Kant 1957, 4)

> For this principle [judgment] is one which must not be derived from a priori concepts, seeing that these are the property of understanding, and judgment is only directed to their application. It has, therefore, itself to furnish a concept, and one from which, properly we get no cognition of a thing, but which it can itself employ as a rule only—but not as an objective rule to which it can adapt its judgment because for that, another faculty of judgment would again be required to enable us to decide whether the case was one for the application of the rule or not.
>
> (Kant 1957, 5)

---

6. See the discussion on this subject by Jonathan Bennett (1974) and by Ralph C.S. Walker (1978).

It would appear that judgment is critical to cognition but is not cognition itself:

> The judgment of taste, therefore, is not a cognitive judgment, and so not logical, but is aesthetic.
>
> (Kant 1957, 41)

Kant then proceeds with an extended treatment of aesthetic judgments. By appealing to a common pleasure principle, he attempts to show that judgment of taste and aesthetic judgments generally can, while springing from the subjective and implying "the objective necessity of the coincidence of feeling," purport to be objective and universal. There is for Kant as well a *sensus communis* which overlaps what we call common sense.[7] The epistemological significance lies in his oblique suggestion that this quasi-intuitive spontaneous act of judgment operates at a deep cognitive level.[8]

But while Kant himself recognized that he was not able to give a complete and satisfactory account of what remained a mysterious faculty, both critiques leave us with two clear perceptions: the first is that judgment may consist in the *application* of a law or rule. Kant says:

> Judgment in general is the faculty of thinking the particular as contained under the universal. If the universal (the rule, principle, or law) is given, then the judgment which subsumes the particular under it is determinant. If however only the particular is given and the universal has to be found for it then the judgment is simply reflective.
>
> (Kant 1957, 18)

---

7. See Hannah Arendt's (1978, 255) treatment of this *Critique*.

8. David Bell (1987) argues that what Kant means by "aesthetic" is not our contemporary sense related to beauty, but a wider sense of spontaneous perception at work in the recognition of the applicability of a rule to a specific instance. Hence the offbeat examples Kant gives of aesthetic judgments: crustaceans, crystals, native tattooing, wallpaper designs. However, at times Kant is differentiating the aesthetics of pure form from form coupled with the fulfillment of an idea as in architecture (a church or summer house).

An example of a determinant judgment is a court rendering a judicial decision on whether a law is applicable to a particular case. An example of a reflective judgment is whether a work of art is beautiful.

Kant's second related insight is that there can be no further principle, rule, or law that tells us how to apply a principle, rule, or law. As he says in a famous paragraph:

> If understanding in general is to be viewed as the faculty of rules, judgment would be the faculty of subsuming under rules, that is, of distinguishing whether something does or does not stand under a given rule. General logic contains, and can contain, no rules for judgment. For if it is sought to give general instructions how we are to subsume under these rules, that is, to distinguish whether something does or does not come under them, that could only be given by means of another rule. This in turn, for the very reason that it is a rule, again demands guidance from judgment. And thus it appears that, though understanding is capable of being instructed and of being equipped with rules, judgment is a peculiar talent that can be practiced only, and cannot be taught.
>
> (Kant 1985, 177)

Kant goes on to say "it is the specific quality of so-called mother wit and its lack no school can make good. . . . Deficiency in judgment is just what is called stupidity" (Kant 1985, 178). Hans-Georg Gadamer comments that as a reaction to this failure of judgment to pass the test of rationality,

> German Enlightenment philosophy considered judgment not among the higher but among the lower powers of the mind. In this respect it diverged considerably from the original Roman sense of *sensus communis* while advancing the scholastic tradition.
>
> (Gadamer 1992, 31)

With Gottlob Frege, writing in the last quarter of the nineteenth century, we arrive at modern times, yet there is something of Kant in his architectonic classification:

We therefore distinguish between:

1: grasping a thought—thinking
2: the recognition of the truth of the thought—judging (*die Anerkennung der Wahrheit eines Gedankens—das Urteilen*)
3: the declaration of the judgment—assertion.

(Frege 1966, 35)[9]

Of Kant and Frege more later.

Ralph Waldo Emerson for all his apparent debt to Montaigne and the rich treatment of Prudence, Manners, Character, and Friendship, is disappointing in his insights on judgment itself. Not so his American successors, the Pragmatists, for whom judgment is process. They focus on the inquiry rather than the conclusion. For John Dewey an assertion without inquiry would not be a judgment, it would be a "mere affirmation," whereas judgment is "the settled outcome of inquiry." Here Dewey is not so distant from Plato in the *Theaetetus,* and in particular the *Sophist*:

> And of these mental processes we have found thinking to be a dialogue of the mind with itself and judgment to be the conclusion of thinking. . . .

(Plato 1982, 1011)

Dewey discusses judgment at some length in *The Quest for Certainty* (1930, 204, 248):

> Intelligence on the other hand is connected with judgment; that is, with selection and arrangement of means to effect consequences and with choice of what we take as our ends. A man is intelligent—in virtue of his capacity to estimate the possibilities of a situation and to act in accordance with his estimate—

---

9. I owe this reference and a discussion to Ernst Tugendhat. My translation avoids attribution of "proposition" and "belief" to "*Gedankens*" and "*Urteilen*." Frege begins his own footnote to this passage: "It seems to me that till now we have not sufficiently distinguished between thought and judgment."

See Tyler Burge (1992) on his full discussion of Frege's notion of grasping a thought.

things are judged in their capacity as signs of other things.—
For if we can judge events as indicators of other events, we can
prepare in all cases for the coming of what is happening. This
conclusion gives intelligence a foothold which reason never
possessed—relatively immediate judgments which we call tact
or to which we give the name intuition do not presume reflective inquiry but the funded products of much thoughtful experience—instead of their being no disputing about taste—they
are the one thing worth disputing about, if by dispute is signified discussion involving reflective inquiry.

For Dewey judgment is part of an amorphous intelligence
without any precise place being assigned to it.[10] Judgmental
processes underlie the whole of his *Human Nature and Conduct*
(1922). Here Dewey moves to a psychological concept of judgment as deliberation with his happy image of dramatic rehearsal:

> Our first problem is then to investigate the nature of ordinary
> judgments upon what it is best or wise to do, or, in ordinary
> language, the nature of deliberation. We begin with a summa-
> ry assertion that deliberation is a dramatic rehearsal (in imagi-
> nation) of various competing possible lines of action.
>
> (Dewey 1922, 190)

Dewey is perhaps the closest in spirit to what runs through
this book. He saw very clearly the estimative elements in judgment and how determinations of weight and relevance affect professional and daily life. But in his enthusiasm to see all cognition
as process and experiment, by seeing logic as a social discipline
(1982, 19) and by depreciating ideas as such, he overshoots distinctions necessary to explain our usage and intuitions with respect to judgment. He never nails down what marks off the exercise of judgment from cognition generally. Dewey's failure to
define the judgmental function as a discrete element in his flux of

---

10. Gilbert Ryle (1949: 285) in "deflating" the intellect (including
judgment) takes Dewey's holistic coping-with-the-environment position
one step farther. For Ryle the process of judgment is "constructed" retro-
spectively after being reached.

inquiry is the more surprising in view of the new light he sheds on instances of its exercise.

It is also surprising that in the writings of another major figure of twentieth-century philosophy, Ludwig Wittgenstein, "judgment" appears so rarely, considering his absorption with neighboring concepts and mental functions. Wittgenstein understood judgment in its Kantian sense of assertion, which fits the centrality of the *proposition* in the *Tractatus Logico-Philosophicus*. In a 1913 letter to Bertrand Russell he admonishes Russell to give up the concept of judgment for the *proposition* itself: "I am very sorry to hear that my objection to your theory of judgment paralyzes you. I think it can only be removed by a correct theory of propositions" (Wittgenstein 1974, 24). Russell took the criticism seriously and abandoned his proposed book on judgment.

In the later subdued Wittgenstein of the *Philosophical Investigations* where he speaks of thoughts, meanings, language games, and rules, it is curious that he would not have strayed to consider the concept of judgment. There is the odd reference for example (1953, no. 488): "How do I judge whether it is so?" David Bell (1987) has pointed out that without actually using the word Wittgenstein picks up on the point made by Kant about the unavailability of rules to interpret rules. Wittgenstein asks:

> Can't we imagine a rule determining the application of a rule, and the doubt which it removes—and so on?

And appears to answer:

> How am I able to obey a rule? If this is not a question about causes then it is about the justification about my following the rule the way I do. If I have exhausted the justifications (i.e., for following a rule in the way that I do) I have reached bedrock, and my spade is turned. Then I am inclined to say "this is simply what I do."
>
> (1953: Nos. 217; 242)[11]

---

11. See Stanley Cavell's cryptic discussion of this famous passage as it relates to Saul Kripke's interpretation of Wittgenstein (Cavell 1990, 72).

David Bell concludes that Wittgenstein implicitly agrees with Kant that "examples are the go-cart of judgment." What remains remarkable is that the later Wittgenstein did not pursue the sense of judgment as exercise, as deliberation.

In his book *Nature of Judgement* Justus Buchler explores from a pragmatic point of view the relationship of judgment to the human condition:

> Judgment is a necessary condition of continuing community, as sheer social togetherness is a necessary condition of judgment.
>
> (1955, 57)

> Judgment is as much appraisal as it is pronouncement. To separate appraisal and pronouncement is impossible.
>
> (1955, 13)

The second passage does focus on the polarity in the concept of judgment as process and decision that runs through its use, both common and philosophical. But, Buchler expands the concept of judgment to embrace all aspects of human activity so that a precise meaning is lost. Anomalously, for Buchler a judgment is essentially a nonmental event:

> The three modes of human production, doing, making and saying, are three modes of judgment that may be designated respectively as active, exhibitive and assertive judgment.
>
> (1955, 20)

Judgment is approached from a quite different direction by George E. Pugh in *The Biological Origin of Human Values* (1977).[12] Coming from a background of computer science, Pugh develops a decision theory based on built-in biologically determined human values. Along the way he gives an illuminating discussion of common sense based on Bayesian logic, which he relates to judgment:

---

12. I owe this reference and a discussion to Anthony Arrott.

Even in discussions that are concerned with objective facts (rather than value judgments) individuals will precede their remarks by phrases such as "in my judgment," "in my opinion," or "my intuition tells me." It is expected that different individuals will have different judgments and different opinions about many factual issues. It is also expected that an 'experienced' individual may have acquired a certain "wisdom" from his experiences that may not be easily explained to justify it. . . . How do these informal concepts of judgment, wisdom, experience and intuition fit into the concept of Bayesian inference? Superficially we might expect that with everyone using the *same* basic deductive method there should be no reason to have differences in judgment. But with a little reflection, it is obvious that this is not true. Even if two individuals were to observe exactly the same process (or even the same sequence of events) the interpretation of events would certainly be different.

(Pugh 1977, 320)

That leaves open the question considered later as to what accounts for the difference in "interpretations." Pugh goes on to postulate the pooling of such individual judgments into a consensus which leads to "wisdom":

Thus the consensus provides a practical way of combining individual experience to achieve a "wisdom" which exceeds that of any single individual. It should be apparent by now that many of the characteristics of commonsense logic are almost inevitable consequences of the requirement for cybernetic efficiency in a finite decision system.

(Pugh 1977, 321)

Gadamer has much to say on the concept of judgment in his essay "Hermeneutics as Practical Philosophy" (1987, 325).[13] There Gadamer invokes Aristotle's concept of *phronesis,* practi-

---

13. Gadamer gives this reference on the meaning of "hermeneutics": "Schleiermacher defines hermeneutics as the art of avoiding misunderstanding" (1976, 7).

cal deliberation or prudence. But he appeals to it not as a spring-board for an analysis of those concepts but rather as an exemplar of a parallel approach to practical philosophy which relies on a corresponding human capacity for achieving mutual understanding with one's fellows. At the beginning of his earlier systematic *Truth and Method* (1992), Gadamer devotes illuminating pages to the history of the concept of judgment but then veers off on a hermeneutic tack. He and others concerned with *interpretation* run together issues respecting that language-centered issue turning on understanding, with judgmental issues that turn on what the mind does with what is understood. Nonetheless, Gadamer is in the forefront of contemporary philosophers in emphasizing the central role in cognition that judgment plays in the application of the general to the particular, discussed later.

Hannah Arendt reaches back to Kant to deal with judgment in her planned work, *The Life of the Mind* (1978). Volume 1 was devoted to "Thinking," volume 2 to "Willing," and volume 3 was intended to be on "Judging." She was only able to finish the first two. After her death a sheet of paper was found in her typewriter, blank except for the heading "Judging." Mary McCarthy, her literary executor, tells us that Arendt thought the subject could be treated shortly as it had remained unnoticed by philosophers except for Kant. She did leave behind illuminating lectures on Kant's *Critique of Judgment* (printed as "Judging" in an appendix to *The Life of the Mind*) in which she touches on various aspects of his thought and sees in them not only aesthetic but political and moral implications. The lectures extend her musings on Kant in "The Crisis in Culture," discussed later (Arendt 1977). Arendt was clearly engrossed by the concept, witness her opening quote from W. H. Auden: "Does God ever judge us by appearances? I suspect that he does."

So we arrive at the present day when judgment as a self-contained subject has received significant contributions from Dewey and Gadamer, has been on the brink of being written about by Russell and Arendt, but, perhaps because of the antipsychological spirit of recent philosophy, has not been dealt with comprehensively head-on.[14] This is particularly so with the aspect of judgment as *exercise*. Yet, it is apparent that any treatment that seeks to clarify the exercise of judgment cannot avoid discussion of the nature of judgment generally. The contributions of philosophers who touch on these matters are discussed later with the subjects treated.

Perhaps it is also because our different uses of the term, readily apparent to the philosopher, appear to break the subject into separate disciplines such as decision theory, aesthetics, jurisprudence, and epistemology, that no attempt has been made to find common logical ground on the way "judgment" works in the language. Nor has an attempt been made to reconcile the different conceptions of judgment which appear to reflect different aspects of usage. Lastly, the central place of judgment in the working of our social institutions, the professions, and our everyday lives has gone largely unnoticed. I attempt to mark out the territory, although it will be for others to map it in detail.

---

14. See Bell (1987, 223) on the interior aspects of thinking and judging: "[A]s a philosophical topic its absence from twentieth-century analytic or Anglo-American philosophy has been conspicuous. This absence might be attributed to the influence of—it has certainly been symptomatized by—the anti-psychologism of both Frege and the author of the *Tractatus,* the behaviorism of Skinner and Quine, the positivism of the Vienna circle, the pragmatism of Peirce and Dewey, and the widespread belief in Wittgenstein's antipathy to all that is private or interior." Significantly, it is not only the *interior* aspects of judging that have been neglected.

II

Elements and Ingredients

Every one complains of his memory, and no one complains of his judgment.

—La Rochefoucauld, *Maxims* (1665)

Sometimes a fool has talent, but never judgment.

—Ibid.

Importance

There is nothing so important in life as knowing what is important. The literature has not shown that this truth is self-evident. Since ancient times there has been talk of value, of knowledge, of truth, but none to my knowledge on importance. While equally foundational, it has lain unattended in the shadow of these glittering and more manageable concepts. It has shared the fate of judgment to which it is closely linked. Importance as the more fundamental idea is an element of and serves to understand judgment.

35

Thus we would not describe someone as having judgment in a certain field if we disagreed with what he finds important in it.

If we start by looking at the most trivial details of our lives, the decisions half-consciously made on which household tasks to concentrate, we realize priorities are assigned which only become evident when they conflict with those assigned by a spouse or child. These priorities are usually set by preferences, wishes, and desires, intuitively understood as subjective. Often, however, the priorities are set by a conscious recognition of what is important. The use of the word *recognition* reminds us that something outside the speaker, his wishes, desires, and preferences is intended. To recognize that something is important is to assign it a structural value which carries an inherent purported objectivity. Recognitions of importance are essential and necessary elements of judgment. Sometimes such recognitions are also sufficient in themselves to constitute judgments. Conversely, we also talk of judgments of what is important.

The objectivity of judgments is manifested in a negative way by observing that life in close proximity with another is only manageable because the dozens of judgments made during the course of the day are shared. This world of shared judgments is an iceberg of which only the tip is occasionally visible. Where the area of disagreement looms large and cannot be reduced to differences in preferences, it poses a threat to maintaining a relationship with the other. Such a person is (if not oneself) at first interesting, later eccentric, then difficult, and finally psychotic.

This immense area in everyday life of coincidence of judgments of what is important goes unnoticed. It is often described simply as common sense—a sense thought common to all in similar circumstances. One way or another our shared background, experience and genetic makeup dictate a wide band within which our day-to-day decisions lie. So seen, what common sense tells us to do is objective. To stray outside the band is intellectually permissible only on occasion and excused by others on the ground of a difference in *values*. The paradox is that the tolerance for different judgments is extended precisely where the *value* component in the judgment is the most dominant extractable ingredient. In such cases where disagreement lies with the moral, political, or other values of the other, it does not cause us to question the other's common sense, only to disagree, perhaps violently. But in the diurnal round, where the value element is largely absent, there is no such tolerance for differences, only a shaking of the head. A socialist and a reactionary have at times cohabited satisfactorily, but two persons who have the same politics but different life styles may find it difficult to do so. And those who have the same political persuasion and the same life styles but can't trust each other's common sense will find it impossible.

Here we should note that common sense (unless it constitutes simply the unexplained residue of cognition) refers to two distinguishable mental processes. One is elementary reasoning, the other the exercise of judgment in seemingly non-intellectual contexts. It is in the latter sense that I use the phrase. Such common sense judgments are in this sense like "perceptual judgments" where unexplained disagreement is equally intolerable. As noted, the level of tolerance for differing judgments is inversely related to the proximity of the subject matter of the judgment to what is commonly called the world of fact. There are inherent conceptual limitations to understanding radically different worlds and conceptual schemes. So it is in a looser way in our daily lives ruled by common sense.

Thus while we are only dimly aware of the scores of sound judgments that make up our day, nothing brings home the central role that judgment plays in our lives more sharply than our distress when we admit to making a bad one. Bad judgments are the phenomenological clincher that legitimizes the concept of judgment, much as falsifying a hypothesis was for Karl Popper a more significant cognitive event than one verifying it. Similarly, J. L. Austin approached the clarification of *real* by asking what we would mean by stating that a duck was unreal, e.g., a decoy. And Schopenhauer's view was that justice can only be understood negatively as the absence of injustice—i.e., injury. So we more readily note bad judgments than good.

Importance vs Values

It is said that the direction our lives take depends on our values. It is less obvious that often in a more direct way our lives turn on our subconscious feelings of what is important. Time and human capacity impose limits that inexorably require countless determinations of relative importance. What kind of school or college is it important that we attend? What courses do we feel are important to take? We find *that* matter interesting because we recognize it as important. Not the other way round. What kind of job we select, what sort of friends we are inclined to make, what area of research we pursue are to a greater or lesser extent governed by intuitions of importance.[15] Again the negative instances are telling. We discard and decline what is not important.

This is most easily seen in individuals directed by defined goals such as status, wealth, academic achievement, and so on. Here there is an easy predicate to "important because———." In these cases the relationship between importance and values is fairly straightforward. Importance works as a metavalue, as a valuer of values.

But more typically a one-dimensional predicate is not readily available to complete the phrase "important because ———." We simply recognize something as important without being able to explain exactly why. It would seem we build up a hierarchy of values that lies deeply embedded in us. The consciousness of the identity of the values dissolves but the skeletal ladder ranking them survives and governs. In this sense, importance serves as a link between a particular decision and an inchoate background of values to be satisfied by the decision. Ultimately our wants, desires, and values use the stepping stone of judgment to lead to action.

---

15. I would put this twist of *importance* on John Rawls's discussion of selecting "rational plans of life" to account for the mechanism: "The potentialities of each individual are greater than those he can hope to realize; and they fall far short of the powers among men generally. Thus everyone must select which of his abilities and possible interests he wishes to encourage; he must plan their training and exercise, and schedule their pursuit in an orderly way" (Rawls 1972, 523).

It may be objected by the skeptical Ockhamite that if importance is simply a link to a scheme of values, why we cannot dispense with importance and proceed directly from the values to the decision. I would suggest that our value system, to the extent specific values are not identified, mediates through the funnel of recognitions of importance which we can bring to consciousness. Our values only become manifest (evident as constructs) by our decisions. The Ockhamite shoe is rather on the other foot. In these cases we feel that our intuitions of importance have a psychological reality whereas the world of values that are presumed to account for them assumes an unknowable status. Indeed, the only testimony to that noumenal world, the shadows on the cave wall, are the individual decisions we take, the judgments we make.

Nevertheless, we can approach an answer to why something strikes us as important. The evening news relates a litany of crimes, traffic accidents, the deposing of the leader of some benighted country. Unless the events touch us personally, they pass us by because they constitute one more member of a class we accept as an unimportant given. But we may attend to the announcement of an arms treaty, a drop in the discount rate, or the overnight collapse of a venerable bank. These are important because significant, and significant because they signify, point to, or possess the potential to change the fabric of our beliefs in a certain area.[16] Or the event may confirm or question a belief that is itself important to us. In recognizing these events as important we are acknowledging their *structural status*. It has been traditional to look on hierarchies as the ordering of values that turn on various narrow meanings of *good*. I am suggesting a shift to importance as the organizing concept. I return to the relationship of importance to values in the last chapter.

---

16. I wish to stay clear of further reference to *significance*. While the term shares the structural sense of importance, it also has overtones of connotation, of meaningfulness that are beyond the scope of this essay. I shall attempt not to stray into that thicket and stick to the structural gist of importance.

Judgments as Kinds of Decision

Having approached judgment obliquely through *importance,* we may now confront the subject head-on. The difficulty in coming to grips with the concept of judgment arises first of all from its reference to several distinct but related phenomena. Judgments are at once kinds of thought (usually but not always deliberation) and results of thought. Here the distinction is between judgment as a kind of decision and the judgmental function implied to have been performed in reaching that decision. The judgmental function may be present yet fall short of a decision being made. On the other hand, the decision once reached can be cast as an assertion which also passes for judgment in certain contexts. Assertions may imply that a judgmental function has been exercised; then again, they may spring full-blown from a dormant belief. Lastly, judgment is thought of as a quality of mind, as a faculty responsible for the judgmental function. All will be treated. But the best starting point is to examine the core aspect of judgment as a kind of decision.

A decision is itself a mental event in which the person deciding commits to one of several alternatives although the alternatives may not always be explicit. The decision may be to carry out some action rather than another or to hold one belief rather than another. When we talk of decision generically we concentrate on the end event itself, and we are unconcerned about how the event was arrived at. One consequence is that although decisions *qua* decisions can be spontaneous, impulsive, or tortured, talk of them carries no presumption of being right. But decisions that constitute judgments, even though quick or snap, imply some confidence that they are *right,* at least in the maker. The justification for this confidence in the judgment being right comes from the implication of the way the decision is reached, the result of a process, however compressed and invisible it may be. Hence the thought or deliberative aspect of judgment. A judgment then is a decision that purports to be right, thus impliedly prescriptive because impliedly the result of a process whose purpose is to make it right. All completed judgments are decisions but all decisions are not judgments.

Where there is particular emphasis on the process by which the judgment is reached, we speak of the *exercise of judgment*. Being a process implies temporality. It may be conscious or it may be *preconscious* in Stuart Hampshire's sense.[17] That is, it can be called into consciousness much as instantaneous translation. The process also implies ingredients, considerations, ways of arriving at the decision which are different from the way a decision is reached which does not constitute the exercise of judgment. For it makes sense to say that someone decided to do something or to believe something, without the decision constituting a judgment.[18]

We saw that judgments are also often thought of as kinds of assertions. That is because the decision that is the end result of the judgmental process is, or can be cast as an assertion. English is ambivalent as to whether a judgment refers to the process or to the assertion in which it culminates. To think of judgment simply as assertion is to miss the distinction between the end point of thought as bare belief, and belief as only one part of a threefold complex (later elaborated) which constitutes judgment. For judgment implies something more and something less than an assertion. Something more, because it implies a preceding process; something less, because of the caution of fallibility absent from a simple assertion. "I judge so and so" stops short of "I know so and so" or simply "so and so." Sometimes the context may supply these qualifications to indicate that an assertion is a covert judgment.

Thus there is in what we recognize as a judgment an implied disclaimer. When we talk of judgment we are alive to its potential rightness or wrongness. Use of "judgment" invites the question as to whether it is correct. So statements we call judgments constitute formulations of decisions which on the one hand purport to be right but on the other hand signal fallibility. As observed earlier, Kant's use of *judgment* in *The Critique of Pure*

---

17. Stuart Hampshire in conversation with Jonathan Miller (1983).

18. It may be said that a generic decision itself presupposes some minimal deliberative process to distinguish it from a reflex. While this psychological bedrock of action and morality has not yielded up its secrets, it is safe to say that there are decisions where the process, whatever it is, stops short of the exercise of judgment.

Reason, where *assertion* would serve, seems strained. Perhaps he is calling attention to the relationship that obtains at a deep level in all cognition between rules and their application, discussed later. Alternatively, Kant, like other philosophers who follow him, may be abusing common speech by using "judgment" where reference to a pragmatically more neutral propositional attitude is appropriate.

So we would not call a statement that five and eight are thirteen a judgment. Nor would we call such statements as "I am sitting on a chair" or "I adore chocolate fudge" judgments. Similarly, it is misleading to call statements such as "I see three chairs in the room" *perceptual judgments.* They do not imply fallibility, are not decisions, and do not imply a process. They are simply statements about perceptions or, better yet, about seeing (or hearing) something. But when I squint and say "I think that's a man on the brow of the hill (and not a bush)" I am going beyond the perception of a protruding object and characterizing it. I may go on to say "I think he's about a mile away." These are examples of estimative judgments which, as Locke pointed out, are often the result of a special skill. They form a subclass of judgments generally. Closely linked to estimative judgments are those half-reflexes we share with other creatures that allow us to dodge mishaps on the streets and the slopes.

Whereas these estimative judgments are the simplest examples of exercising judgment, examples at the other end of the spectrum range from the diagnosis of an obscure disease, to a judgment handed down by a court, to a budget tabled by a government where the temporal element will be protracted. And in between there is the fabric of our everyday lives that represents the calculus of innumerable judgments made each day. Perhaps the most ubiquitous example lies in our speech, in our choice of words and how we say them. The richness of our language offers many alternatives. Each will have a different effect on the listener or reader. While each will have a different meaning, the concept of meaning drops out and the judicious speaker or writer will aim straight for the effect. She will achieve it by choosing this formulation rather than another. Although such exercise is the stock-in-trade of the politician, the lawyer, and the writer, it is present to a degree in all human intercourse.

Beliefs and Intentionality

Judgments spring from beliefs and issue in beliefs. It is therefore appropriate to consider judgment in the context of belief. It is said that judgments, like beliefs, assertions, declarations, and so on are propositional attitudes.[19] That is, the initial verb that uniquely expresses the sort of "attitude" followed by a contained sentence results in the form *A judges that P.* Judgments being sorts of decisions are, however, episodic whereas at first blush beliefs do not appear to be so.[20] W. G. Lycan and other philosophers hold that beliefs, in contrast to judgments, are mental states. But what is a mental state? Lycan's answer is given in terms of disposition, itself a conundrum.

It has also been said that belief is like a stroll which implies an ongoing activity. But belief is not like a stroll. We think of belief in two ways. The first is the root concept of a conscious (in the sense of a then seemingly acknowledged) mental event: I *believe* in this sense only if I BELIEVE.[21] The force of the expression "led to believe" is to bring the respondent of the Socratic method or of an effective cross-examination to experience such an event. In this sense belief is episodic and "real," but in a different sense than

---

19. An expression, I believe, coined by Bertrand Russell (1962, 62) and in common use since, although with reservations by Davidson as "attitudes directed (as one says) upon propositions" (Davidson 1980, 230).

20. See W. G. Lycan's discussion of the relationship of judgment to belief in his promisingly titled *Judgment and Justification* (1988).

21. Robert Nozick seems to acknowledge such a psychologically real state for he asks the rhetorical question: "But why is it necessary to *believe* any statement or proposition? Why not simply assign probabilities to each and every statement without definitely believing any one and, in choice situations, act upon these probabilities by (perhaps) maximizing expected utility? Such is the position of radical Bayesianism, and it has some appeal" (1993, 94). Nozick ends up rejecting this position.

that of Jerry Fodor who appears to lump it in with pain and other sensations.[22] Admittedly, we are left with the residual indeterminancy as to what is going on when we are aware of *holding* a belief.[23] Perhaps the closest we can come is to see such an event as an inner voicing, sometimes articulated. There remains an air of unreality in pressing the psychological distinction between occurrent belief, holding a belief, and judgment as terminal belief, beyond acknowledging a common event element.

However, clearly we usually talk of beliefs in a second sense where they are not consciously held in the mind with no apparent event element. This expanded derivative meaning depends on our assumption that once the believer has held the root belief, she would express it if provoked. Such attribution of belief is therefore a construct which we impose on the believer. Common sense and the courts rightly attribute beliefs where there is convincing evidence to conclude that there was belief in the first sense. Attribution must be cautious; it would be odd and unfair if the evidence indicated the witness had never held such a belief in the first sense.

This penumbra which radiates beyond conscious belief covers gaps in content as well as time. There is an analogy with sight. We look across the street at a building. Counsel then asks, "Well, if you saw the building then you must have seen the open window on the top storey and the mountains behind, correct?" At some point you invoke the concept of notice and deny the imposition by saying "I didn't notice it." So with beliefs. If we didn't realize the logical implication from one belief to another, we can rightly say we didn't believe that thought. "Led to believe" means what it says. We therefore do not need concepts of tacit or implicit belief, or belief as an ongoing state of mind. We can make do with beliefs as episodic mental events, as past episodic beliefs stored in mem-

---

22. See Daniel Dennett's (1988) references and citations to Fodor.

23. Although I am not here concerned with the debate about whether beliefs are in the mind, beliefs in my root sense would appear to be so just as other mental events, while beliefs as constructs are imputed to the mind. But what beliefs are directed to, propositions, are not in the mind because they are not the sorts of things that are *in* anything. See footnotes 26 and 140. See also John Searle (1994).

ory, and as constructs that we attribute to those we believe believe. Admittedly, *state of mind* is a handy shortcut to refer to the expectation of the recurrence of similar mental events (disposition) as long as its expository value is not taken too seriously. This schema of belief sketched out here cuts across the realist views of Jerry Fodor and the opposing views of Daniel Dennett of beliefs as abstracta (Dennett 1988).

To return to judgment, it is these first-order beliefs that we turn over in our minds or are at work preconsciously as we deliberate in the formulation of our judgment. Archetypal judgments seen as decisions radiate no such penumbra for they are site specific. Here it is appropriate to refer to the discussion of judgment by Davidson in two articles, "Intending" and "How Is Weakness of the Will Possible?"[24] The brief treatment of judgment is peripheral to his explication of the relation of intention to action. Judgment is therefore not dealt with comprehensively, only to the extent it bears on action through the concept of intention. Davidson distinguishes between *prima facie judgments* (my eating something sweet is desirable) and what he calls *all-out judgment:* "forming an intention, deciding, choosing and deliberating are various modes of arriving at the judgement, but it is possible to come to have such a judgement or attitude without any of these modes applying" (1980, 99). For Davidson, intentions "constitute a sub-class of the all-out judgements, those directed to future actions of the agent, and made in the light of his beliefs" (1980, 102). His all-out judgments appear to correspond roughly to what I simply call judgments. Davidson would probably agree that not every all-out judgment results in or is intended to result in action. Some, perhaps most judgments, lie fallow as belief.

I differ from Davidson on what he calls prima facie evaluative judgments. He classes wants and desires as examples of such judgments, but being conditional on the effect of the surrounding circumstances, they are starting points in the deliberative journey to all-out judgment that will serve as an intention to perform a certain act. While wants and desires are certainly starting points and ingre-

---

24. Both published in *Essays on Actions and Events* (1980).

dients in reaching judgments, to refer to them as prima facie *judgments* is to overlook that all judgments imply the making of a decision which wants, desires, and attitudes do not. So *holding* a value is itself not a judgment but a decision *to hold* a value is. In a footnote Davidson recognizes that *judgment* "is not necessarily appropriate to express wants and desires" (1980, 97).[25]

Earlier I discussed the relationship between values and judgments and I characterized judgments as stepping stones between wants, desires, held values and beliefs to other beliefs and actions. It is this path indicated by Davidson that is explored here. And I take up consideration of the distinction he anticipates between judgment and other propositional expressions of attitudes by delineating in these pages the features that distinguish it. One such distinction is raised by Dennett (1988, 114): "Can one make a judgment without believing it? Is there such a phenomenon as unconscious judgment (a puzzle within folk psychology)?" The answer to the first question is surely no, for the reason that, on the view advanced here, judgment is in part decision and in part the belief that issues from it. The second, I believe, is answered by invoking Hampshire's *preconscious* referred to a few pages back. The demands of clarity allow us to push these distinctions only so far before usefulness gives out.

What judgments do have in common with beliefs—indeed seen as end points they are beliefs and propositional attitudes[26]—

---

25. The caution is well advised. "Want" hides two different goings-on. There is the want in "I want to rumple your hair" and there is the want in "I want peace in Bosnia." Only the second can be translated as "I want *that* there be peace in Bosnia."

26. Intentionality marks a divide masked by the casual use of "propositional attitude" to describe all manner of relations between mental events and propositions. Intentionality appears in full force in beliefs. As Marcia Cavell (1993, 10) observes, beliefs are precisely tailored to individual propositions. Thus the belief of Oedipus that he killed a man at the crossroads is different from the belief that he killed his father there. So it is with the derivative concepts of knowledge and judgment. But contrary to Cavell, I believe it is otherwise with affectively tinged "attitudes" such as hopes and wants, which go straight to a state of affairs only roughly rendered by a proposition. Put another way, there is an indissoluble *logical*

is their directedness toward something beyond themselves, the proposition encapsulated in the contained statement *P.* That is their intentionality or *aboutness.*[27] This directedness is caught by Wittgenstein (1988, 135) in a rare reference to judgment:

> For judgment too has its psychology. It is important that we can imagine every judgment beginning with the words, "I judge that ———." So is each judgment a judgment about the one who is judging? No, it is not—as I don't want the main consequences that are drawn to be ones about *myself,* I want them rather to be about the subject matter of the judgment. If I say "it's raining" I don't in general want to be answered "So *that's* how it seems to you." "We're talking about the weather," I might say, "not about me."

Here Wittgenstein displays a tacit acceptance of Kantian and prevalent philosophic usage since. For, the odd example chosen, "It's raining," although a graphic example of belief and intentionality, is not what in common speech we would call a judgment (no process, no decision, no fallibility). Second, it misses mention that this propositional attitude does not float quite so free from ties to its agent as do others ("I know") that express intentionality. This is the force of Frege's remark, cited later, that "we do not know the act (of judgment) if we do not know the agent." There is here a fork in the road between philosophers such as Kant and Wittgenstein, who do not seem concerned about the distinction between judgment and assertion, and the position argued here that it is critical.

---

link between a belief and the proposition, whereas the content of a wish or want depends on the mental facts. Psychology may or may not equate "I wish that the coffee cup is full" with "I want a full cup of coffee." This is faux intentionality.

27. See also John Searle (1983, 1): "Intentionality is that property of many mental states and events by which they are directed at or about or of objects and states of affairs in the world." See the many aspects of intentionality discussed by Davidson (1984) and the opposing positions of Fodor (1978) and Stalnaker (1984) on this central issue. Far more profound even than the question of what it is to think rationally is the question of what it means to think *about* things at all.

What runs through these writers is the common assumption that judgment is logically one-dimensional, simply a propositional attitude. The key to seeing its singular place in the language is to realize that judgment is logically complex; its three aspects—process, decision, and belief—are present to a degree in all its cognate forms. We saw that judgment could best be approached in its aspect as a sort of decision. Decisions are themselves not propositional attitudes. We say "X decides Y," not, "X decides that Y." We say, "X decides that P is true," where the whole noun clause embracing P constitutes Y, not P alone. So, we say, "John decides that the sentence 'It is raining' is true." Here the whole clause, "that the sentence 'It is raining' is true," constitutes the object of the decision and not the proposition, "It is raining." Decisions are episodic events, mental acts, in a sense that attitudes aren't. But as judgments, they are directed to and issue in beliefs. Thus, it is only this final residual aspect of judgment that can be described as a (considered) belief and thus a propositional attitude.

Judgment as Process

Having considered judgment in its core aspect as decision and gone forward to consider it in its resting place as considered belief, we now go back behind the decision to examine the third aspect implied by judgment. For as we saw, *exercising* judgment is the process directed to making such a decision.

That is not to say that the order of decision and process cannot be silently reversed. We often reach a tentative decision half conscious of the parameters that will shape it. We then struggle backward to construct considerations and reasons to justify the judgment and its implications. That such a grounding process is available and can be replayed is of the essence of judgment. Take two sorts of judgment apparent in the legal process. One is to make a judgment to believe this witness rather than the other. If pressed, the judge or juror may come up with reasons—consistency, demeanor, confidence, and so on. In this sort of judgment the looseness of the recital of reasons is tolerable. The second sort of judgment is the court's decision on the issues, which does raise expectations of a credible construction of reasons for the decision. Judgments imply an inherent potential for a degree of articulation of the process.

When we say that someone has judgment or exercises judgment we mean, of course, good judgment. And when we say good judgment we do not mean a judgment that turns out to be haphazardly right. We imply something about the process by which it was reached regardless of the outcome. Plato's dialogue of the mind with itself must precede the conclusion to constitute it a judgment. But it is the peculiar form of this dialogue that we call the exercise that we allude to when we talk of the resulting conclusion as a judgment. To be sure, a judgment is said to be "proved" correct if it is borne out by future events. Such proof is indirectly taken to be relevant to assess the quality of the process and the judgmental faculty of the judge. Nonetheless, as we shall see, "good judgment" is an attribution of a mental quality independent of particular consequences, of individual successes and failures.

What then are the essential factors of this process? Can we isolate those mental functions that examples of good judgment have in common? At the outset we should exclude from consideration the faculties of intelligence and reason essential in some measure before judgment can come into play. It is noteworthy that tests have been devised to measure, therefore quantify, these faculties. But the ability to judge has defied measurement and perhaps for that reason has not qualified as a self-contained quality of mind worthy of inclusion in the pantheon of philosophers and psychologists.

Here it is appropriate to consider work done in two branches of psychology that touch (but only just) on judgment. One is recent research on intelligence, particularly practical intelligence. The other is work in cognition, particularly decision theory. I will deal here with the recent work on intelligence and leave the discussion on cognition and decision theory to my later remarks under "Judgment as Prediction."

Judgment and Intelligence

Recent work on intelligence has focused on expanding the concept in various ways to account for achievement in life that cannot be accounted for by a standard IQ test. Howard Gardner and Joseph Walders have proposed a theory of multiple intelligences.[28] They define intelligence as an ability or set of abilities that permits an individual to solve problems or fashion products that are of consequence in a particular cultural setting. More precisely, that is their definition of an Intelligence. They then proceed to postulate seven intelligences: musical intelligence, bodily kinesthetic intelligence, logical-mathematical intelligence, linguistic intelligence, spatial intelligence, interpersonal intelligence, and intrapersonal intelligence. One would have expected treatment of the exercise of judgment and the special elements referred to later by me in this very broad approach. Curiously, the exercise of judgment is only treated tangentially and implicitly by referring to certain tasks that assume the exercise of judgment.

Another significant work in this direction is by Robert Sternberg, particularly in *The Triarchic Mind* (1988) and by some twenty-three psychologists in *Practical Intelligence* (Sternberg and Wagoner, 1986). The writers put forward various definitions of intelligence such as speed of information processing, the capacity for learning, forms of competence, and the ability to deal with novel demands. There is disagreement among the authors as to whether these concepts of intelligence describe an underlying quality of mind to explain why some people are better at some tasks than others or whether they simply fulfill a descriptive role that provides a general characterization of the performance to be expected in a broad range of tasks on the basis of sampling in that domain. The latter is the position taken by David R. Olson, who suggests that a problem in the conceptualization of intelligence is the confusion of description with explanation, a warning that is applicable to all conceptualizations that tend to reify what is mere description. Surprisingly again, judgment is not explicitly consid-

---

28. Walders and Gardner (1986).

ered. This may flow from a recognition that intelligence, even if broadly defined, is in some sense a prior quality of mind to be marked off from judgment, with which I would agree.

So the literature on intelligence does not take us much further in understanding judgment. It traverses the controversy whether IQ tests have limited application to a certain socioeconomic context. There is a recognition that the narrow conception of intelligence underlying such tests captures the ability to comprehend matters relating primarily to language and numbers or more comprehensively, *pattern recognition.* Along with pattern recognition we can think of intelligence as the sheer computerlike ability to keep in the mind and manipulate numerous levels of abstraction. Judgment on the other hand can be seen as the ability, in part, to impose degrees of relevance and weight to these levels to apply them to the case at hand.

Within such a context there appears to be a positive correlation over a broad statistical range between intelligence as measured by IQ tests and professional and academic achievement. However, no convincing answer emerges to account for large individual variations in performance within wide bands of IQ results. Herrnstein and Murray argue in *The Bell Curve* (1994)[29] that there is strong evidence that intelligence as understood in IQ tests is a necessary condition of success in cognitively demanding fields. But it is not a sufficient condition. I depart from the literature in arguing that in many cases the sufficiency is in large

---

29. My comments on *The Bell Curve* are confined to noting that the authors use "intelligence" and "cognitive ability" interchangeably. They equate the two (p. 22). Remarkably, judgment is not discussed. Where does it fit in? If it is part of cognitive ability, the authors' conclusions of measurability and heritability would need be applied to judgment, a conclusion not apparently supported by present evidence. If, on the other hand, the authors believe that judgment, as here described, is not part of cognitive ability, then how to explain the large role judgment plays in aspects of cognition? We cut the knot by seeing that cognitive ability is not undifferentiated. Cognitive ability is intelligence plus other things. The argument that runs through this book is that judgment is one such. This differentiation has large implications on the measurability and heritability of cognitive ability as commonly understood.

part supplied by the ability to exercise judgment. We are aware of highly intelligent people who are notorious for making bad judgments, even in their own field of expertise. We often remark that notwithstanding someone's intelligence or rationality the person lacks judgment. We have our favorite examples. There is the person of quick and ready understanding who occasionally misses the import of some critical fact, or cannot size up the significance of a course of action, or does not heed Aristotle's caution in the first cited passage on the appropriateness of standards. What requires investigation by psychologists is whether the capacity to exercise judgment has a parallel status to the capacity measured by IQ tests, whatever that status may be.

Other writers who take the notion of intelligence beyond the narrow limits of the IQ test do not deal, except peripherally, with the elements of judgment isolated here. What appears useful is to restore the concept of intelligence to what is roughly captured by the IQ tests. It does not follow that the notion of cognitive ability need be confined to such a narrow concept of intelligence. Breadth is added by judgment. Within any such context it makes sense to say that intelligence does not imply judgment. There is intuitive plausibility and anecdotal evidence that support isolating judgment as an identifiable mental function or faculty placed somewhere between intelligence and character, although touching both. In referring in a folk way to this capacity for judgment as a faculty, I am mindful of Olson's caution not to reify or attribute explanatory power to what is a mere description. I thus part from Dewey and many others who think of judgment as part of intelligence.

It is also a commonplace that a prodigious store of knowledge does not imply sound judgment. Knowledge in this sense means knowing what, not knowing how. Knowing how is closely related to judgment. We sometimes use the expression "skilled at deciding so and so" interchangeably with "he is a good judge of so and so." Whether such a skill is due to learning or to a natural aptitude presents a challenge to empirical investigation. There appears to be a learning element in being able to pick out the critical features of a special field, in being alive to highlights, in discarding the irrelevant. Yet what remains to be explained is that if this aspect of judgment is a skill acquired through learning and experience, why some, including those in the professions, do not acquire it in spite of lifelong exposure.

Judgmental Attributes

Some sections back we began to isolate the mental qualities essential to good judgment. While a certain level of intelligence is a precondition, it was seen not to be an element of judgment itself. Rationality will be distinguished later. Imagination is another such essential mental quality which may precede judgment. It is against a background of these first order faculties that judgment as an identifiable bundle of second order mental qualities and functions is to be distinguished.

The first quality in the bundle is attitudinal. There must be a commitment to arrive at the *right* decision and not one which is merely pleasing. Closely connected to such a commitment is the ability to abstract oneself from the matter being judged. There must be an inner commitment to achieve such objectivity and impartiality. That is because a judgment by definition purports to have objective validity, if only to satisfy the personal needs of the judge. Being objective is a code word for a complex, attitudinal state understood negatively in terms of not permitting personal considerations to intrude on the judgmental process. There is no need to embrace a belief in absolute objectivity or deny that we impose structures on the world to recognize different degrees of objectivity in those around us. Much of what Ronald Dworkin (1985, 171) calls interpretation is in effect judgment. Interpretation is a special kind of judgment on what a text or speech means. But that said, he is right that the objectivity of interpretation and judgments generally cannot be taken beyond the worth of the arguments for or against. Objectivity can also be understood positively—of taking the outside world seriously, of staring reality in the face. So seen, it is a strong brand of intentionality. By an absorption with aboutness, about what is out there, it puts to one side the claims of what is in here. It can be stretched or heightened in social and judicial contexts by considering the issues from the point of view of those involved.[30] In our capacity to stand above and outside a problem, to see it in its context, we recognize a connection between this ingredient, essential to judgment, and *character,* explored later.

Given the objective stance, there are two other qualities of mind that are critical. The first brings us back to *importance*: the capacity to get to the heart of the matter, to recognize the essential features in a situation. It is impossible to exercise judgment without having a sure sense of what is important in the matter at hand. As we saw, importance is the chief (the most comprehensive) of the bundle of concepts of which *essential, key, central, elemental, salient, weighty,* and *prior* are also members. Every case of judging involves focusing on the issues, that is, identifying the elements. The capacity to recognize what is important thus implies a predilection to structure, to hierarchy. Whether empirical study can illumine this cast of mind is provoking.

Behind the concept of importance stands *relevance.* All matters which are important must be relevant although all relevant matters may differ in importance. There are an infinite number of similarities and dissimilarities between any two things in the world.[31] Most of these are trivial; that is an indication of how far

---

30. For a perceptive account see Lynn Smith's article in *The Advocate,* January 1987, in which she discusses "Heightened Objectivity" as the state of mind of a judge when considering cases of disadvantaged minorities:

"The approach to decision making which I will call 'heightened objectivity' is that which is not only dispassionate and disinterested but also has three other characteristics:

1. a rigorous disregard for common assumptions and expectations about people deriving from their membership in particular groups;

2. an exercise of the power of the imagination, to consider an issue from the perspective of those involved even though that perspective may be very different from that of the decision maker; and

3. an exercise of the creative and analytical faculties, in asking whether the law itself is skewed by history built upon preconceptions about particular groups or disregard for their perspective."

31. See the work of R. Shephard and P. Podgorny (1978) on judgments of similarities and comparisons.

logic departs from common sense, which tells us that only certain similarities or dissimilarities are relevant to a decision and it is only the relevant features that qualify to be considered important. Psychologists Keith Holyoak and Barbara Spellman (1993) have reviewed the extensive literature, particularly as it bears on the role of relevance to inference, the conventional constraints on the use of "if" and the influence of context on reasoning.

What is relevant in turn is critical in determining what constitutes evidence, or potential evidence. One position in the literature introduces the concept of *background information* to define evidence which in turn relies on relevance. As well, anything is evidence for a hypothesis if it makes the truth of that hypothesis more probable.[32] It follows from both positions that if something is evidence, then it must be relevant. The meaning we give to relevance in everyday discourse is prescriptive: any consideration we should take into account in reaching a decision. The same mental processes are at work in recognizing relevance as in recognizing importance, except that relevance is a binary concept: either a matter is relevant to an issue or it is not. Again, a structural approach is at work that isolates and ranges the constituents of an issue.

Appropriateness

Side by side with importance is the other quality of mind (the most elusive yet most characteristic) critical to judgment, a feeling for *appropriateness* or fit. At the lowest level, a candidate for decision is implicitly tested for fit with other beliefs, that is, for consistency. Further along it is what is commensurate. While logic may suffice to determine consistency, to get from consistency to appropriateness requires judgment. In the paradigm cases of judgment where appropriateness looms large, the tests become subtle and approach the domain of taste. Here judgment is required to determine appropriateness where mere consistency

---

32. See the discussion in *Mind* between Peter Achinstein and Maya Bar-Hillel and A. Margalit, January 1978, October 1979, January 1981.

leaves off. We recognize its ubiquitous presence in our use of language. We think of a happy phrase or *bon mot*. Less conspicuously, our everyday discourse is molded by consideration of the appropriate choice of words. It is tempting to add "to reflect our thoughts." Whether such addition is justifiable depends on our philosophical position on the relationship between language and thought. Of course, mostly we do not choose our words at all. They tumble out without reflection, without judgment. What is clear is that the appropriateness of the words we end up using as a result of deliberation has a profound impact on our relations to the world and the relations of others to us.

While the form our personal language takes is the most pervasive example of appropriateness, it is starkly present in all events of social moment. Social relationships depend on the continuous exercise of judgment by the participants, of minute adjustments to conduct, usually through language, made by determinations of importance and appropriateness. It is the lapses that give a glimpse of the iceberg.

In a more obvious sense of appropriateness we think of a sentence imposed by a court on an offender. We think of the reaction of a leader (the measured, calibrated response) to the downing of an airliner, to hostages in an embassy, or to the assassination of an archduke where making the *in*appropriate statement or taking the *in*appropriate action can affect the course of history. In the commercial world, there is the response of a chairman to a product failure. At lower levels there is the consideration of the appropriateness of compensation levels, although to apply this criterion to salaries of entertainment and sports figures would be to commit a category mistake. With respect to many of these judgments we find ourselves using the expression *getting it right,* also apt to the span of creative acts. These range from a hairstyle, a herbaceous border, a musical phrase, to a point made in debate, and a bit of literary criticism. All acknowledge that the criterion of appropriateness is to be met, that judgment need be exercised.

A vivid example of the centrality of appropriateness in public life is the budget-making process in parliamentary systems. There (as against the United States, where budgets are not born fully formed), budgets are sprung on the public by a majority government that does not require to negotiate their substance. But because of their significance as political symbols, they are crafted with an eye to the appropriate degree of appeasement to domestic constituencies, quieting foreign concerns, and signalling long-term goals. The public's first reaction is, "Have they got it right?"

"Getting it right" does not only mean arranging the internal parts appropriately but getting it right with respect to background. It means attending to context, balance, and perspective. In pruning roses the severity of each cut depends on a series of internal relationships, a judgment made with respect to each cane or shoot. One then stands back to survey the bed, to bring external relations into line. More generally, context is not restricted to the sort of facts discussed in relation to evidence but to the frames of expectation with which the individual and others (to satisfy the claim of objectivity) come to the problem. This is what Aristotle is getting at in the passage first cited; different subjects and different contexts deserve different treatments, a consideration that we shall see is critical to the professions.

But the separation between importance and appropriateness and between the qualities of mind to detect them is by no means watertight. For determining appropriateness itself involves identifying the relevant and important features. It also implies selecting the salient features from the context. So we come back to the concepts of importance and structure. And a person who has a feel for fit is the one sufficiently removed from the subject to have a wide view of the surrounding country, who sees things in perspective, which takes us back to objectivity. While objectivity, importance, and appropriateness are interrelated, they point to different aspects of a cast of mind committed to reality. When we lift the lid off cases of judgment, we discover determinations of importance and appropriateness at work.

Earlier we sought to distinguish intelligence from judgment. But here, too, there are no watertight distinctions. Intelligence has been thought of as pattern recognition as can the feel for appropriateness. But with intelligence we think of *recognizing* internal patterns in a given conceptual space whereas with appropriateness we think of *appreciating* a pattern between the subject and its wider external background, of placing a new particular into the existing general. There is micro-internal pattern recognition as against macro-external pattern appreciation. Pattern recognition in intelligence seems content to rest with a passive perception, whereas pattern recognition in judgment is the result of an active determination. When we think of what is appropriate, indeed what is *fitting*, it is hard to banish images grounded in sense perception, the slotting-in of the piece in the hand, what complements a scene, what doesn't jar the ear. A capacity for the first sort of pattern recognition does not appear to guarantee a capacity for the second.

It will not have escaped notice that there is a regress in determining what is appropriate and what is important. Subsidiary judgments of appropriateness and importance may be called for. It may be objected that appropriateness and importance are not bedrock concepts because it makes sense to ask "appropriate or important for *what purpose,* what end?" Appropriateness and importance are thus pushed back to such other criteria. Acting reasonably means following that trail as long as it remains discernible. I would argue that when the markings fail we are left with the phenomenological end-point that a certain factor is recognized "in the circumstances" as important or appropriate (or more typically as *un*important or *in*appropriate) *tout court.* It is recourse to our everyday experience—that ultimately we simply recognize certain conduct as right or wrong—which grounds intuitionism in ethical theory. Parallel ingredients are present in recognitions of importance and appropriateness. It is perhaps this regress, this dark alley, that has scared off analysis.

III

Contrasts and Distinctions

We should be gentle with those who err, not in will, but in judgment.

—Sophocles, *Trachiniae*

'Tis with our judgments as our watches: none go just alike, yet each believes his own.

—Alexander Pope, *An Essay on Criticism*

Judgment and Rules

We saw in the last section that in determining importance or appropriateness a person may well ask the question, "Important or appropriate for what purpose?" There may well be a ready answer to such an appeal in which event the inquiry is satisfied. On the other hand, the appeal to purpose or other criteria may lead to a further appeal to the concepts of importance and appropriateness. This reference to purposes and criteria may be thought of as appeals to rules that work as normative constraints to determine the decision. Philip Pettit has defined a rule as follows:

> A rule is a function which can take an indefinite variety of decision-types as inputs and deliver in each case one option— or set of options—as output: this is the option that is identified as the most *appropriate* in some way. [Emphasis mine]
>
> (Pettit 1990, 3)

Recent philosophical discussion has been much concerned about the role of rules and rule following in language and thought (Kripke 1982; Boghossian 1989). Rules function explicitly in etiquette, morality, and games, but also implicitly on the applicability of abstractions such as universals, concepts, or properties. Apart from the normative character of the rule, Pettit, commenting on Saul Kripke, names three other elements in order to qualify: the rule must be determinable or identifiable; it must be directly readable; and yet, paradoxically, it must be fallibly readable. That is, the rule follower, while being able to tell straightaway what it requires, does not thereby obtain an epistemic guarantee that he has got the requirement of the rule right.

The fallibility referred to by Pettit is of a more narrow order than the one I referred to earlier that inheres in all uses of judgmental language. The fallibility I referred to derives from the casting of statements as judgments rather than as unqualified assertions. This is most obvious where we see judgments as stand-ins for knowledge. It is of course true that reading off a rule does not carry with it any epistemic guarantee of being right. Indeed, this is hardly surprising in the light of the mystery of what is involved in being able to read off or follow a rule at all, even in the directly readable way. As we saw, it was Kant's great insight that judgment is the art or faculty of applying a concept or rule to a particular case. This insight, when coupled with his other that there is no rule to which we can appeal to test its application, is of a piece with the recognition of the fallibility of judgments in Pettit's sense.

Rule-following takes place on several levels. Some hold that at the deepest level it is involved subconsciously in every application of a universal to a particular. Does the event warrant the application of "red" or "chair"? Whether rule-following is involved in this way is beyond my scope. But the fact that in a standard case we have no doubt that the application of "red" or "chair" is right and that this is about as infallible an attribution as one can get, casts doubt on the usefulness of the appeal to rule-following (or indeed perhaps to rules themselves) or to judgment in such case. While a judgmental *function* may be involved here, English usage would not sanction reference to judgment because no process or decision is involved. At such a deep level we can say that if indeed there is rule-following, the rule can simply be "read off." Judgment enters at an obvious, superficial level with respect to applying articulated rules governing conduct. At an intermediate level are the rules for the application of terms like "negligent."

Now, how this account of rule-following relates to the sort of judgmental process that I am discussing is this: where such rules can be directly read off, a judgmental function is not involved except possibly at the deepest level. But in all other cases judgment comes into play precisely because one has come to the end of the rule-following game. Perhaps there is no available rule to fit the unique kind of event. More often rules can accommodate too much material. As is noted later under the section titled "Courts," social rules are open-textured. They are expressed in language necessarily loose whose meaning is always susceptible to various "interpretations." Here judgment is required to choose the right interpretation; that is, to apply the rule correctly in the circumstances. So it appears that contrary to these writers, rules are not always "directly readable"; judgment is often required to read them.

Finally, we need to emerge from considering the obscure role of the judgmental function in rule-following to confront its obvious role in determining when a rule is *not* to be followed. Thus the stuff of any professional practice consists in knowing when not to follow a rule, policy or principle. It is counterfactual to insist that in such a case there is always an appeal to another, higher rule.

Judgment as Prediction

When we term a decision a judgment, an implicit question is being asked to which that judgment is the answer. There must therefore be alternative answers. Each answer will have a certain degree of *probability of being right*. This expression is most easily understood for judgments that can be "proved" right by future events. Judgments of this sort therefore involve attributing probabilities both to ingredients in the process of arriving at the judgment and to the judgment itself. Here we see at work two different uses of "probable": the probability of a statement being true, of an answer being right (truth probability) as against the probability of a future event taking place (event probability).[33] The distinction is put differently as subjective (or personal) probability and objective (or statistical) probability. Subjective probability is then further divided into *actual* belief and *rational* belief.

> Once we recognize that decision theory needs the subjective concept of probability, it is clear that the theory of *actual* decisions involves the first version of this concept, i.e., the *actual* degree of belief and the theory of *rational* decisions involves the second version, the *rational* degree of belief. . . . The concept of probability in the sense of *actual* degree of belief is a psychological concept; its laws are empirical laws of psychology to be established by the investigation of the behavior of persons in situations of uncertainty, e.g., behavior with respect to bets or games of chance. . . . I shall use for this psychological concept the technical term "degree of credence."
>
> (Carnap 1960, 303)

While the two concepts are clearly distinct and while truth probability or degree of credence is the relevant issue in understanding judgment, event or statistical probability will have an effect on the former. Attributing an event probability may in turn require identi-

---

33. Rudolf Carnap's somewhat different early formulation was *degree of confirmation* and *relative frequency*; see "The Two Concepts of Probability" in *Readings and Philosophical Analysis,* eds. H. Feigl and W. Sellars (New York: Appleton-Century-Crofts, 1949).

fying and tracking causal relations in order to predict consequences. As discussed later, judgments in politics and commerce involve determining particularly complex causal relationships.

Because event probability lends itself to quantification, this aspect of judgment has attracted considerable attention in the literature. Work has centered on inference. An attempt has been made to use Bayes's Rule to link events and hypotheses in a simple or serial way. The rule holds that we can judge between alternate hypotheses simply by asking which one provides the most accurate prediction about a system. Contrary to mathematical theories of probability, Bayes's rule or theorem provides that the relative likelihood of one hypothesis against another is altered by the outcome of events or by a conditional piece of evidence. In other words, empirical results affect the next set of probabilities.[34]

George Pugh (1977) maintains that the human brain works much like a computer that can be programmed as a value-driven decision system. Such a computer would compare alternative courses of action and select one that seems "best" in terms of a built-in system of values. Much like the human mind, it makes valuative and judgmental decisions. The trick is to program the computer with the right desiderata or criteria of value and to assign numerical weights to these. He goes on to contend that these primary values have been built into the human brain (prewired) through biological evolution and that these primary values, which are akin to our fundamental biological instincts, determine our sec-

---

34. See Margaret Matlin (1983). Matlin defines Bayes's rule as requiring that the judgment of the relative likelihood of two events depends on the *base rate*. The base rate is the proportion of the matter in question in the relevant population. She cites the extensive work by D. Kahneman and A. Tversky on how such judgments are made. Curiously, in this comprehensive textbook on cognition explicit reference to judgment is almost wholly absent. Indeed the standard texts on cognition hardly refer to judgment except in relation to Bayes's rule. R. C. Jeffrey (1983, 1) has a broader concept of Bayes's rule: "The Bayesian principle, then, is to choose an act of maximum estimated desirability." Still another definition of the rule is given by Gregory Currie (1993, 423): "the probability of an hypothesis *H* on given evidence *e* is equal to the likelihood of the hypothesis times the prior probability of the hypothesis all over the prior probability of the evidence."

ondary values. The theory does not answer how or why we attribute weights to secondary and tertiary values, or how we arrive at our everyday judgments (particularly those turning on appropriateness) that seem far removed from values of any sort.

The emphasis on Bayesian inference placed by Pugh in human judgment is closely related to the theories of other writers that move away from mathematical probability in analyzing rational decisions. They emphasize the close connection between prediction and judgmental qualities. Jonathan Cohen cites John Maynard Keynes's view that weight cannot be analyzed in terms of mathematical probability since the relation between A and B in p [B, A] = n is unchanged regardless of the weight of A. Keynes speaks of the *weight* of evidence in discussing practical inference:

> One argument has more weight than another if it is based on a greater amount of relevant evidence. . . . It has a greater amount of probability than another if the balance in its favor, of what evidence there is, is greater than the balance in favor of the argument with which we compare it.
>
> (Keynes cited in Cohen 1977, 36)

Cohen argues in favor of a concept of inductive probability based on a grading of provability which he contends underlies judicial proof.

Lofti Zadeh and the proponents of fuzzy logic have gone beyond Bayes's theorem in their disenchantment with mathematical theories of probability. Zadeh's example is of a typical graph that plots the probability of first-time marriages of women at different ages (lecture at the University of British Columbia, October 12, 1991). The probability of a woman in her early thirties getting married for the first time is indicated at, say, 9 percent. But what relevance does this have in determining the probability of such a marriage of a particular woman at that age? Clearly, the probability applicable to her will be determined not only by her age but by her looks, her health, her social position, her friends, her means, and indeed by her entire background, which are not capable of statistical generalization or computerization. Zadeh concludes that it is not safe to venture beyond

imprecise verbal concepts such as "high" and "low." It is the gap
between statistical predictability of trends and the unpredictability of a particular movement that is exploited by fuzzy logic. The
Japanese, who are not hampered by the Cartesian mindset for
certainty, have enthusiastically embraced fuzzy logic to design
control mechanisms of all manner of technology.

Chaos theory, a related development, attempts to draw some
meaning from the seeming anarchy of natural and social events.
But even if the chain that leads from the particular flapping of a
butterfly's wings to a tornado on the other side of the globe were
theoretically predictable, the flapping itself or its human analogue, the particular individual action, is not.[35] We can more confidently predict that our sun will spend its hydrogen fuel in, say,
five and a half billion years than whether the girl in the next aisle

---

35. See James Gleick's comments on cosmologist Stephen Hawking:

Yet Hawking recognized that understanding nature's laws on the
terms of particle physics left unanswered the question of how to
apply those laws to any but the simplest of systems. Predictability
is one thing in a cloud chamber where two particles collide at the
end of a race around an accelerator. It is something else altogether in the simplest tub of roiling fluid, or in the earth's weather, or
in the human brain (Gleick 1987, 7).

A wry human example is given by Trotsky, the arch historical deter-
minist. As is well known, Trotsky was incapacitated by influenza from
attending Lenin's funeral and from defending himself against Stalin in the
struggle for succession:

One of the Sundays in October, 1923, found me in Zabolotye, on
the bog, among the reeds. There was a slight frost that night and I
sat in the tent in felt boots. . . . The moment I stepped onto the bog
in my felt boots my feet were in cold water. . . . The cold got the
better of me. I had to stay in bed. After the influenza, some cryp-
togenic temperature set in. The doctors ordered me to stay in bed,
and thus I spent the rest of the autumn and winter. This means that
all through the discussion of "Trotskyism" in 1923, I was ill. One
can foresee a revolution or a war, but it is impossible to foresee the
consequences of an autumn shooting-trip for wild ducks. (Leon
Trotsky, *My Life* [New York: Pathfinder Press, 1970], p. 498)

will pick up her pencil in the next five minutes. Yet predictions and judgments are made about individual actions nonetheless.

It is tempting to reduce all judgments to a tracing of causal links and thus to prediction. This critical role of causal tracing is brought home by reflecting on how often misjudgments stem from fingering the wrong cause in the mix as decisive. After all, if judgments are simply complex predictions of alternative outcomes, we can dispense with the troublesome concepts of importance and appropriateness. And perhaps appropriateness can be reduced to predictions as to how event-patterns fit together and the reactions (other event-patterns) to them. Similarly, perhaps utility can be reduced to the probability of positive mental states.

Certainly there are cases of judgment where prediction appears to exhaust the analysis. Importance still holds as the paramount criterion, but weakly. Take the case of choosing the quickest check-in line at the airport. Here judgment passes through the concept of importance—what key factors to take into account—straight to a causal analysis. Will the foreign couple in this line cause as much delay as the excessive baggage in the next? But even here there is ultimately a weighing of the ingredients as there is in archetypal judgmental questions:[36] What course should I

---

36. The question of weight always present in the law in assessing the value of evidence has recently spread from evidence to substance. In determining whether there was liability for negligent misrepresentation the court cited with approval:

Professor Blom suggests that mere foreseeability is insufficient to found a duty of care for negligent misrepresentation; there must, in his view, be something to establish an undertaking on the part of the person imparting the information. At pp. 293–94, he states:

We all rely routinely on many things we are told, without being justified in assuming that some legal liability would attach if the information turned out to be negligently given. The question is not so much whether a reasonable person would rely, as whether a reasonably prudent and skeptical person would think that the information or advice carried conviction, not only of its quality, but also of a certain legal *weight*.

take? Whom should I believe? What policy should I advocate? In a broader sense even than Keynes intended, when we think of judgment we think of weighing: weighing of priorities, weighing of consequences, weighing appropriateness, weighing these considerations against each other, and weighing the probabilities themselves.[37] Note the etymological connection between "weight" and the German words for weight (*Gewicht*) and important (*wichtig*). In turn, there is an irreducible *salience* (important, appropriate) element to the concept of weight.

The weighing process is recursive because the determination of each element itself may require further weighing, further judgment. While theory dictates a regress, psychological fact points to the petering out of a rigorous process early on. One measure of rationality is the dogged pursuit of that path until it becomes too faint to follow further.

Decision Theory

The most extensive work applying probability to decisions is in cognitive theory. We noted that in the other relevant branch of psychology dealing with intelligence there was rare reference to judgment. In decision theory, judgment, if not front and center, at least rates consideration. A comprehensive survey of the literature begins:

> Judgment and decision making are topics that for many years have stood apart from other areas of psychology. They are presumably facets of human information processing and part of

---

(*Kinqu* v. *Walmar Ventures Ltd.* 10 B.C.L.R. [2d] 1986 per McLachlin, J.A., quoting Jost Blom, "The Evolving Relationship Between Contract and Tort," *Canadian Business Law Journal* 10 [1985]: 257.)

37. Sometimes we reach back from judgments to weights given to certain considerations. The judgments of some car manufacturers to install driver-side but not passenger-side airbags makes a statement on the weight given the psychological state of the surviving driver whose passenger was killed.

the larger field of cognitive psychology. *An informal survey of current textbooks suggests however that if the study of judgment and decision making is an important part of cognition, the fact is not widely recognized.* [Emphasis mine]

(Pitz and Sachs 1984, 139)

The flavor of the approach taken by these authors is given by the following excerpt:

A judgment or decision making (J.D.M.) task is characterized either by uncertainty of information or outcome, or by concern for a person's preferences, or both. Unlike other tasks, there may exist no criterion for determining whether a single choice or judgment is correct, since the response is based in part on personal opinion or preferences. It is possible, however, to impose a mathematical or logical structure on the task that defines the consistency of a set of responses. The prescriptions for consistent behavior are generally derived from formal probability theory and from expected utility (E.U.) theory, a prescriptive model of choice founded on axioms proposed by Von Neumann and Morgenstern. Bayesian decision theory (e.g., Raiffa and Schlaifer 1961) is a prescriptive theory of choice based on a combination of probability theory and E.U. theory. The validity of these prescriptive models as descriptions of human behavior has for many years been a dominant theme in this area . . . *numerous authors have demonstrated that judgment departs significantly from the prescriptions of formal decision theory.* [Emphasis mine]

(Pitz and Sachs 1984, 140)

What is apparent from the literature is that explanatory models are inadequate to explain more than the most elemental kinds of judgment, those that can be structured as, and reduced to, a given preference and probability which can be quantified. Even highly sophisticated formulations of these rules have been found inadequate to describe the complex inference in natural settings such as the courtroom or the operating room (Schum 1977). While the writers provide insights into a multitude of judgmental ingredients and construct a rough calculus of rational procedure, the concepts that we intuit to be at the heart of the judgment, though recognized, are left to one side. For example, Pitz and Sachs refer to weighing:

> In spite of the widespread use of averaging models, not much is known about the cognitive determinants of the weighing process. Weights are often considered to be a function of the *salience* of problem features (Shantau & Ptacek 1983) but such an account partly begs the question and is to some extent misleading. [Emphasis mine]
>
> (1984, 151)

Credibility and salience are brought in by N. J. Castellan in considering decisions as information processing:

> The information-processing capabilities of people are characterized as a multistep or hierarchical process. The stimuli or cues (or information) are broken down into components for processing. In the chapters by Wallsten and Castellan this is accomplished by describing the cues in terms of aspects and dimensions, respectively. In Schum's chapter, the evidence is divided into components representing the *credibility* of the information source and the inferential or *diagnostic* value of the testimony. Further division results from consideration of the testimony of multiple sources.
>
> Each author makes different assumptions about the manner of combination of information for processing. Wallsten's model assumes that subjects attend to sources of information in terms of their *saliency,* the most salient source being examined first, followed by the next most *salient* dimension. Evaluation of information continues until the criterion level of certainty is reached at which time the subject will stop seeking information and make a response. Castellan also describes a model of *selective* attention. In his model, the subject attends to dimensions in a probabilistic fashion such that attention is focused on dimensions in proportion to their validity. [Emphasis mine]
>
> (1977, 86)

Apart from the inherent problem of weight or salience referred to in the above passage, judgments are conditioned by two other indefinable factors: *context* and *similarity*. Pitz and Sachs write:

> The growing interest in cognitive mechanisms is the result of two sets of findings: the changes in judgments that occur as a function of changes in the way a task is presented (Payne 1982), and the observation that people use simplifying heuristics to deal with complex judgment tasks. These findings are interconnected; many demonstrations of task-dependent results, such as the effect of the "framing" of a task on judgments (Tversky and Kahneman 1981), show that the invariance demanded by prescriptive models is not present. What is significant for a cognitive psychologist is that the *context* in which a judgment is made affects that judgment.
>
> (1984, 145)

> The use of existent information to derive further propositions about the problem is the basis for inference in a J.D.M. task. The most frequent accounts of the inference process rely on the concept of "representativeness," a term that Tversky and Kahneman (1982) define as a relation between a hypothetical process and some event associated with the process.
>
> For some problems the perception of representativeness is mediated by judgments of similarity, for example, the *similarity* of a personality description to a general stereotype. *It has proved as difficult to define similarity satisfactorily as it is to define representativeness.* [Emphasis mine]
>
> (1984, 149)

Tversky and Kahneman summarize their findings on the effect framing has on preferences and choices:

> The psychological principles that govern the perception of decision problems and the evaluation of probabilities and outcomes produce predictable shifts of preference when the same problem is *framed* in different ways. Reversals of preference are demonstrated in choices regarding monetary outcomes, both hypothetical and real, and in questions pertaining to the loss of human lives. [Emphasis mine]
>
> (1981, 453)

Judgment needs be imported not only in answering the particular question put, but in deciding how it should be put—what is
the appropriate frame. For decision theory then, on at least three
counts—weight, similarity, and context (including framing)—
judgment is thus explainable only in terms of other judgments.

Judgment and Reason

The remarks a while back on rationality remind us that the
boundary between judgment and reason is blurred. Both are
processes relevant to cognition. Both proceed as a secondary
process from the primal illumination thrown up by intelligence
and imagination. Reason deals with connections, with determining whether one thing follows another, which it may take intelligence to recognize. The series may follow a deductive or inductive path. Reason admits of criteria by which such a progression
is validated. The norms of rationality such as noncontradiction
differ from and precede the norms of judgment. By contrast,
judgment is informed by the concepts of weight, importance and
appropriateness, which are not capable of being definitively validated. While both are normative, judgment has a direct judicial
function absent from reason. That is, judgment *rules* on alternatives whereas reason reads off a logical sequence. But usage indicates a crossover by such derivative words as "reasonable" and
"rationality" whose meanings point to both processes. The
process of clarifying our thoughts, of getting clear about an issue
is in part antecedent and incidental to both reason and judgment.
Judgment assumes reason has been employed where necessary
along the way. While reason considered narrowly does not
assume judgment, judgment is required to determine what sort of
reasoning or logic is appropriate in the circumstances: strict
inference, Baysean inference, or fuzzy logic. We are reminded by
Aristotle in the passage first cited that it depends on how much
precision is appropriate, how much *im*precision we and the subject can tolerate. In general, judgment is superimposed on rationality seen narrowly, a subject treated further in the last chapter.

There is another use of "reason" to distinguish. Admonitions to listen to the "voice of reason" or to "let reason prevail" endemic to issues of social policy are essentially calls to modify "logical" positions by factors outside the logic: to see things in perspective, to take stock of what is important, to bring other considerations to bear and attribute appropriate weights to them, in short to exercise judgment.

These matters come to the fore where environmental, planning or aesthetic concerns come into conflict with economic demands and property rights. Here we are accustomed to see confrontation of extreme positions expressed in ideological slogans: no clear-cutting of the forest, no commercial development, no high density, no relaxation of zoning. While these positions may be politically expedient, they are often self-defeating for the ideals they champion and may not do justice to them. Because environmental and planning policies should seek tangible results, site-specific solutions are called for.

This implies a different decision procedure to achieve political ends (where slogans and principles may be useful in altering public attitudes and political direction) from the procedure demanded by such site-specific issues. These require answers to questions of *how* rather than *what,* where the claims of form do not so much supersede substance but become substance.[38] The right solution will seldom fit under an accessible formula or slogan. It must be painfully achieved by dealing with each case on its merits. So approached, the *reasonable* solution may even accommodate claims perceived as adverse. In all this, when we ask the last necessary question, "Does it make sense?" (the very question neglected by those lacking judgment), we are appealing to recognitions of importance and appropriateness beyond the borders of any discipline or logic.

---

38. An explicit recognition in the law that in some cases "form is substance" appears in the dissenting opinion of Esson, J. A. in *National Trust Co. Ltd.* v *Bank of Montreal et al.,* a complex commercial case discussed in footnote 55 below.

Practical Reasoning

I said at the outset that one of the implications of accepting the centrality of the judgmental function was to see what has traditionally been written about practical reasoning in a new light. While the territory thought to be covered by that heading is not entirely clear, it seems to cover deliberation to determine what action to take. Kant and Hume through their absorption with reason and reasoning dealt extensively with the place of these concepts in determining action. Later writers hived off the area of reasoning leading to conduct under the heading Practical Reasoning, as does Robert Audi (1989). He follows a consideration of Aristotle, Hume, and Kant with his own position, a variation of a belief-want model of explanation and justification of action. Most work on practical reasoning, like its more mathematical twin, decision-theory, turns on this model: a rudimentary motivational element ("I want X"), a cognitive element ("because my doing A will contribute to, or cause or have the probability of realizing X"), and a decision element ("I should therefore do A").

The burden of my argument is to cut across the sort of analysis undertaken by Audi and stay clear of the bevy of technical arguments that distinguish between the

> *correspondence thesis* according to which for every intentional action there corresponds at least one practical argument whose premises express motivation and belief jointly sufficient to explain the action and *inferentialism* according to which every intentional action is based on reasoning, even if tacit which expresses an argument to which it corresponds.[39]

Audi discusses practical reason in terms of *practical* judgments answering *practical* questions. But what are practical judgments and practical questions? To the extent the expression simply marks out the territory of the subject matter, such a rough demar-

---

cation is legitimate. But Audi adopts the traditional position that there is a structural difference between practical reasoning and theoretical reasoning. It is said practical reasoning tells us what to do, theoretical reasoning tells what is true. But that in itself does not raise any such distinction in principle. Indeed, since what we believe is true plays such an important part in what we decide to do, this ground taken by itself is suspect.

The first thing to note about the distinction that marks off practical reasoning is that common speech does not recognize it. We don't talk of "practical reasoning." We decide what to believe or what to do, we ask why someone did something and we consider the reasons given. Reasoning narrowly conceived is simply logic, whether strict, Baysean, or fuzzy. Conceived broadly it covers the whole range of human cognitive processes. Means-to-end reasoning is employed to determine not only what to do but also what to believe. Inserting wants or beliefs into major/minor premises does not change the structure of a syllogism.[40]

It is common ground that what goes into intentional action involves one's desires and beliefs. But how illuminating, except in the simplest instances, is it to construct a formula: X wants Y, X believes that A-ing is required to achieve Y, X determines to do A and does A? I say "construct" because what is required is to hypothesize Y as a want, desire, or goal. There are such simple cases but these are rarely the ones where any reasoning (practical or otherwise) goes on. They may lend themselves to the familiar risk/reward formula. Like fording a stream in hip waders, you take one stone at a time with an eye on the riffles. It works pretty well if the water is clear and you can see the stones. In these sorts of cases it seems closer to psychological reality to say that the motivating desire proceeds straight to the action. My argument is that the line should be drawn after this class of cases.

On the other side of the stream are the more complex cases where judgment is involved because the water is muddy. Here no simple formula will serve, at any rate not one that has any psy-

---

40. See Davidson's discussion on G. E. M. Anscombe's denial that the practical syllogism is deductive (Davidson 1980, 9).

chological validity. For what justification do we have to hypothesize a want? We ask ourselves, do I really *want* Y? Do I want Y more than Z? What are the implications of wanting Y? Ought I to want Y? How appropriate is it to do A? We may put "wanting Y" on a pedestal, a position that it occupies fleetingly. For a moment the syllogism applies, then the computer screen flashes a different set of permutations. Is the want sufficiently definable to be fit for logical manipulation?[41] Should we not challenge the autonomy of wants as raw givens in precisely those situations where the analysis is worthwhile? For wants take on their shape in the judgmental process.

Ultimately we make a judgment to do X because X is the right thing to do. This is a belief we hold true, which is the reason, shortly put, for our doing the act. We see what has traditionally been described as practical reasoning leading necessarily to beliefs, that is, to a cognitive, theoretical result. All *deliberation* leading to action passes through the gateway of belief, of which judgment is the guardian. By placing beliefs front and center, we destroy the distinction between practical and theoretical reasoning. It is what the beliefs are about and what they may lead to that differentiates.

That is not to say that actions cannot proceed directly from wants (which may at a deeper level themselves house embedded beliefs) without passing through judgments of "what is the best thing for me to do." Recognizing that the process is sometimes through judgment and sometimes directly to action is the beginning of an explanation of incontinence, weakness of the will, or *akrasia*. In fact the puzzle of incontinence only arises on the

---

41. Francis Fukuyama (1992), tracing a line from Plato through Hobbes and Hegel, has deconstructed wants by splitting off non-natural desires under the head of *thymos* which he sees as desire for recognition responsible for much of human conduct: "The self-assertive nature of *thymos* leads to the common confusion of *thymos* and desire. In fact, the self-assertion arising from *thymos* and the selfishness of desire are very distinct phenomena" (Fukuyama 1992, 172). I would suggest Fukuyama's thymos is readily subsumed under Spinoza's more comprehensive concept of pleasure as the feeling of increase in one's power.

assumption that such a judgment is present in the incontinent action. No judgment, no incontinence or inconsistency to explain away. What seems to happen is that where judgment is present, the agent judges X the best course but the motivational force of his desire for Y simply leads him directly to doing Y (usually a primary want in the sense distinguished in footnote 25) because that force overwhelms any motivational force that accompanies his belief that he ought to do X. This explanation is not far from Hume's position except that for him (as for Hobbes) the force of one desire simply beats out the other without necessarily assuming the presence of any judgment in my sense.[42] The position sketched out here is also consistent with Hume's notorious phrase, "Reason is, and ought only to be, the slave of the passions" (*The Treatise,* p. 415). For Hume can be understood to mean that there is only one sort of reasoning process, and that it is employed intermittently as a tool in an extended judgmental process to link wants and beliefs. Recent works on Hume touch peripherally on the role of judgment in thinking. Annette Baier gives the following summary of Hume's position,[43] which accords with much I say:

> Our capacity for judgment outruns our capacity to reduce our judgments to rule. We trust our powers of judgment more than we trust our ability to generalize about what determines our judgment.
>
> (p. 281)

---

42. The moral domain has no monopoly on incontinence. Take the problem of choosing the best lane in rush hour traffic. There is a long line behind a stop light in the curb lane and a much shorter line in the center lane. You *know* that probably at least one of the cars in the center lane wants to turn left and the probability of getting through the intersection quicker is clearly to stay in the curb lane. Yet your aversion to being at the end of a long line will, time and time again, make you take the center lane—to your regret. How does this humdrum case fit S. L. Hurley's (1989, 136) elaborate structure of *prima facie* and *pro tanto* reasons to explain *akrasia*?

Nor does literature have a monopoly on *aperçus.* There is no reason to believe that poetic insights into the human condition are inherently distinct from those in business, science, or the everyday.

43. As quoted by Kretschmer (1993, 348).

For John Rawls "[t]he definition of the good is purely formal. It simply states that a person's good is determined by the rational plan of life that he would choose with deliberative rationality for a maximal class" of plans (1972, 424). Rawls starts out following Henry Sidgwick's notion of deliberative rationality but prudently backs off somewhat from conceding success to the strategy:

> His choice may be an unhappy one, but if so it is because his beliefs are understandably mistaken or his knowledge insufficient, and not because he drew hasty and fallacious inferences or was confused as to what he really wanted.
>
> (Rawls 1972, 417)

Rawls does not back off enough. Surely what really happens is not a plan that goes wrong because *knowledge* is insufficient but because innumerable judgments of importance and appropriateness defy description as a rational plan.

Audi also gets it wrong in his interpretation of the Antigone legend. Antigone, contrary to the order of Creon and the law of the land, determines to bury her brother Polyneices as required by the demands of religion. Audi sees this as an example of one rule overriding another rule to serve as the major premise in the practical reasoning that leads to the action. The force of the example is rather to highlight the complex interplay of emotions, reasoning, and questioning that lies behind the anguished decision which proceeds from what she determines in innumerable ways is *appropriate* and supremely *important* to her that displaces any consideration of rules. It is not the surface decision (seen externally as a construct of one rule overriding another) but the subterranean lode that is mined by the dramatist and psychologist.

John Broome (1991) misses this indeterminancy of identifying one's own good in his approach to utilitarianism using the methods of economics. By positing certainties not grounded in psychology, his maneuvers take on an air of unreality. After all, the existence of preferences (Broome's *goods*) is itself not immune to question. He invokes the metaphor of weighing to account for the aggregation of good and bad features of an act but without appeal to the concepts of importance and appropriateness stressed here as central to the weigh(t)ing process. Thus he is confronted with the problem of incommensurability where weighing in its narrow sense comes to a halt in the face of incompatible categories. Yet that is precisely where weighing must come in. Polls show that voters trust one presidential candidate more than another but think the other is more competent. After Watergate trust was more important; in a recession perhaps competence is more appropriate.

Gilbert Harman in explaining practical reasoning clings to an ideal rationality, yet so watered down that it belies the name:

> In general, no particular reasoning is absolutely required by rationality at any given time. Ordinarily, any of a number of different changes in your antecedent view might be acceptable. You are not forced to reason in one way only. You might reason this way or that way or the other way. . . . There is no more evidence that there are explicit general principles of reasoning than there are explicit general principles of aesthetic appreciation.
>
> (1977, 129)

I suggest the process is something like this. We deliberate about what we should believe or do. As Harman recognizes, the presence of words such as "should" indicates choice. But the further insight is that the process may require innumerable subsidiary choices along the way to the ultimate judgment. These subsidiary decisions are judgment nodes strung together by recognized reasoning procedures. The fact that the resulting web can be laid out for appreciation is a necessary condition for rationality. But it is not sufficient, for, as will be discussed later under "Rationality," the critical nodes remain opaque.[44]

Judgments on Principle

What is said about reason can be expanded to decision procedures generally by noting the asymmetry between ready-made

---

44. S. L. Hurley's contribution to this issue is discussed in the last chapter under "Rationality."

concepts and what is called for by the particular case. Hence, judgments often go wrong from a misconceived adherence to principle. A certain decision is rejected because it is inconsistent with a principle or methodology or because it is deemed to be *ad hoc* or expedient. Yet such decisions are often right. The flaw lies in not recognizing that acting on principle is rarely a virtue in itself. A principle is often no more than an abbreviated, dressed up form of a decision procedure estimated to produce the right result most of the time. Reliance on such a general guide may give a false sense of security to a decision that ultimately must stand on its own feet, that is, be justified by factors outside the principle. And conceptions themselves live precariously on the edge of being done in by the infinity of variables.

The resistance to taking a decision inconsistent with a methodology or principle is often due to a reluctance to undertake a fresh causal or logical analysis combined with a hesitancy to deviate from a comfortably embraced procedure. Principles and methodologies by their nature lead to categories of desiderata rather than to specific defined events. Thus there is greater precision in determining probabilities relating specific means to specific desiderata rather than deducing such means from principles, methodologies, or rules, which in itself is a risky enterprise. The probability of error in derivations from plan or principle (assuming the appropriate one has been selected) may well be greater than the probability of error in proceeding directly to the judgment. In an article on John Reed, chief executive of Citicorp, the *Wall Street Journal* (August 16, 1991) quotes him as follows:

> He now talks of running Citicorp like a New Age industrial company with thin layers of management, peer-review evaluations, far fewer meetings, and "judgments" replacing a lot of three-year plans "that no one ever looked at anyway."[45]

---

45. This nod to the practical value of judgment is a forerunner to what is being called the reengineering of management governance to distribute decision making (judgmental responsibility) non-hierarchically throughout the organization.

A common mistake encouraged by undue reliance on rational structures is to disregard the margin of error inherent in most of them. The confidence in the result cannot exceed the margin of error in the judgmental underpinnings. Thus can an elaborate argument be toppled by a slight judgmental shift.

How far one takes a principle is itself a matter for which no decision procedure can be prescribed. Some rules are to be taken more seriously than others. It depends on the circumstances, on what is appropriate, that is, on judgment. It is the badge of a judgmental issue that no step-by-step derivation from principle is available. Paradoxically, if the matter is of little moment, principles and conceptions provide an effective shortcut. So if we see a shabby figure in a dark alley, *pre*conceptions and even stereotypes are there to fall back on. Closely related is the convenience of "executive decisions." These are designed to flow without further thought from a ready-made, comprehensive judgment to avoid the bother of decisions at each instance. So, an investor's judgment not to reply to the bombardment of proxy solicitations results in filing them unopened in the wastebasket. On the other hand, we are also familiar with the functioning of small groups where rules of procedure are left in the background in the interest of getting things done, and those that insist otherwise are considered a nuisance. In more serious matters danger flags are flying when principles harden into ideology to become bullet-proofed against judgment. We need not accede to Paul Feyerabend's (1978) iconoclasm "anything goes" to recognize by a different route that methodology is hostage to the demands of circumstance.

We are aware of the danger of labeling and generalizing that language necessarily requires. If we are truly concerned to describe a subject accurately, we expand and particularize. So it is with principles, a species of generalization. They are a starting point, but when it counts we do not take them or the limits of their extension for granted. Where a considered belief or action is in point, then so is judgment. We examine our grounds for, and consequences of, holding principles and, if required, redefine. But if that is so, are we in the end arguing from the principle *to* the particular decision or *from* the particular decision (otherwise arrived at) to the principle?[46]

Moral decisions are implicated accordingly. It is not only an intellectual virtue to see things as they are, to judge on the merits. The fallout of adopting a principle in a particular case is what counts. It is consequences and the intended consequences of the particular act that are morally relevant. This leaves open the debate over what sort of consequences are at stake. The Categorical Imperative urges one grand set, Utilitarianism another. But as Ivan Karamazov dramatizes it to his brother Alyosha, the universal effect of a decision, even the saving of the world, is still to be weighed against the significance of an isolated monstrous act.

This regard for immediate concrete consequences drifts into an emphasis on means and in turn on all aspects of the act, some being decisive. Gandhi took this position to an extreme, as recounted by Ronald Duncan on the first words he heard after travelling from England to meet the Indian leader at his ashram:

> "As I was saying in my last letter," he began before I had time to dust the tonga off my back, "means must determine ends and indeed it's questionable in human affairs whether there is an end. The best we can do is to make sure of the method and examine our motive. . . .
>
> "Every act," he would repeat almost daily to me, "has its spiritual, economic, and social implications."[47]

Of course this teleological skepticism may, by its reference to motive, hide a commitment to elusive ends. How are these to be cast? Nowadays people shy away from talking of ideals, they prefer principles.[48] Yet the frames of principle inhibit free judg-

---

46. See R.M. Hare's (1952, 70) discussion of decisions of principle in relation to moral conduct: "to make a value judgment is to make a decision of principle."

47. Ronald Duncan, *The Writings of Gandhi* (London: Fontana & Collins, 1983), pp. 12, 19.

48. Nozick (1993) heads his first chapter: "How to Do Things with Principles."

ment whereas ideals are points approachable from many directions. Ideals themselves are attenuated normative considerations
which in turn are the generic feedstock of judgment. Being right
may be too important not to remain open, to the extent allowed
by our human limits, to a zero-based strategy of examining all
approaches without hindrance.

Further, there is a trap built into a reliance on principles.
There is always a question lurking called for by their logical status, an implicit demand to complete the structure, for ordering,
prioritizing, and reconciling. The search for a talisman has been
all but abandoned. But the nagging question is banished by moving both up and down. Up, so that the positive thrust behind the
principle is cast as a diffuse ideal, and down, to the concrete judgment into which the ideal enters. Within clusters of ideals as distant lodestars, conflict becomes academic. Within the judgmental
process, it is doubtful that empirical study would show that historically right decisions were arrived at by a calculus of principles. What is suggested is that determinations of importance and
appropriateness enter in an opaque way. It is after the event that
one engages in rationalization.

Judging Judgment

The question skirted so far is what is meant by expressions such
as good judgment. Three different attributions of value to judgment can be distinguished.

The first describes a judgment as right or correct in the sense
that the judgmental decision is proved right by future or outside
events. Even though judgments speak of what should be done or
believed in the present they point to the future, to consequences,
to outside events that would have affected the judgment had the
judge known of them when the judgment was made. We estimate
a distance at 500 feet. A future measurement proves us right or
wrong. In this sense our attribution of value to the judgment
depends solely on such outside events.

The second attribution of value is to the person making the

judgment. We say a person has good judgment or is a good judge of, say, people. We must be mindful that we here use "judgment" to denote a quality of mind rather than a countable event. Two things are involved here. One is a record of having made individual judgments that were proved right in the first sense above. A person comes by a reputation of having good judgment by arriving at judgments that in the main coincide with judgments of those who judge him. In addition, while coincidence of judgment is often the simplest test by which we attribute good judgment to another, it is often not unique and even absent. For we say that someone has good judgment even if it does not always coincide with our own if we approve of the way the judgment is made. I may go into a partner's office to discuss a thorny problem; I hear her out and I may accept her conclusion because of the way I observed her reaching it. Or I may not agree with the conclusion but still respect her judgment. This leads to the last distinction.

The third sort of attribution of value then is to the judgmental process itself. Does it make sense to talk of sound judgment regardless of its result—that is, valuing the judgment apart from its correctness in the first sense? By focusing on the process rather than the result we deprive ourselves of a measurable test of the quality of judgments. From that point of view judgment as a faculty becomes inherently incapable of measurement in contrast to the measurement of other faculties such as intelligence and memory. This follows from noting that every exercise of judgment is tailor-made to fit a particular set of circumstances. Thus criteria cannot be specified in advance, only matters to be kept in mind. To the extent the ingredients in a judgment can simply be read off, the process itself becomes a perception or a calculation and not a judgment. This has profound implications for the susceptibility of judgment to artificial intelligence discussed later.

Judgments in this third sense cannot be judged by some external factor, but only by regarding the internal process. Were the right issues identified and considered? Were the right priorities attached? Was it reasonable in the light of the then known facts to attach the probabilities given to the alternatives. Was the result appropriate? All are further judgments themselves. Does the fact

of easy victory in the Gulf War make the judgment of those who
warned against it wrong?[49] Again, it will be easier to spot a lapse
in the process than conformity.

Drawing the Elements Together

At this point we should remind ourselves of the distinction
between getting clear about the use of "judgment" in everyday
speech and examining the judgmental function itself. We saw that
our use of "judgment" implies decision, process, and fallibility
yet prescription. From this point of view, using "judgment,"
where mere declaration, statement, or assertion will serve, is to
abuse the language.

I have also attempted to illumine the judgmental function
irrespective of the use of terms. We saw that the simplest example of this function was estimative judgment such as estimating
distance, recognizing a triptych as by a certain Lowland Master,
or attaching credibility to the testimony of a witness. In each case
the skill consists in giving correct answers under less than optimum conditions where the answers cannot be read off as the
results of infallible perception. The broad application of the
expression *to take the measure of* something indicates how estimative judgments have served as paradigms for others.

In more complex cases we saw that the exercise of judgment
involves the following elements: maintaining an objective attitude, framing the right question, identifying degrees of importance, making Baysian inferences, forging logical links, and test-
ing the steps along the way and the putative answer for appropri-

---

49. Herodotus tells of Artabanus warning Xerxes against invading
Greece. Artabanus takes the line of valuing the judgmental process rather
than the result to its extreme, observing that if in spite of lack of planning
and judgment the enterprise should nonetheless succeed, "Well, that's a bit
of luck indeed, but he still has the shame of knowing that he was ill-pre-
pared." John Broome points out (1991, 126) that G. E. Moore held the
opposite view: "goodness and rightness must depend on what would actually happen, not what you expect to happen."

ateness to the context. Our purpose for making the judgment enters the process indirectly. Why are we making the judgment? With respect to beliefs it may simply be for the satisfaction of knowing the truth. With respect to actions it is to reach some desirable result. The process may involve working backward in a causal way from the desirable end and determining how best to achieve it. The causal analysis will involve probability judgments that may lead us to proceed by counterexample, by rejecting alternative courses of action. When our activities turn out wrong, our first claim to innocence rests on not having any way of taking the cause into account.

I have attempted to relate the various conceptions of judgment. We have Plato, Frege, and Dewey, who think of judgment as the conclusion of thinking, the settled outcome of inquiry. For Kant it seems to be the assertion itself with an implied string to the assertor. But it is also the faculty that mediates between rules and instances of application. Others think of judgment as the giving of an informed opinion on some issue. Still others distinguish between theoretical judgments that are a type of fact-stating claim requiring special talents or skills and practical judgment as to what should be done (Audi 1989; Baier 1958). Locke in his brief quoted passage perhaps comes closest to capturing our everyday use of judgment as a stand-in for knowledge. Dewey is also present here. Aristotle led the way in his emphasis on judgment as *exercise* with the underlying emphasis on the concept of appropriateness, of which only a whiff is present in Plato, Kant, and Frege. But even they, in concentrating on the affirmation of the truth of an assertion, could not avoid a reference back to the process that got them there. Accommodation if not reconciliation will be attempted in the last chapter.

The view put forward here is that judgments are logically distinct from propositional attitudes such as knowing, and indeed cannot properly be taken at face value as such attitudes. The core aspect of decision looks back to a deliberative process and forward to a belief. Judgment implies a process, an act, and an attitude. Regardless of form or use, the threefold nature distinguishes the meaning of "X judges Y is wrong" from "X believes Y is wrong."

Beyond logic, judgments can be seen as kernels of commitment that answer an implied question. The answer purports to be objective yet is recognized as fallible. The answer implies determinations of importance and appropriateness, or both. Importance bears on determining the pertinent causal or structural connections which in turn may lead to determinations of probability. To take an idea seriously denotes not only volitional attendance, but the making of a judgment that the idea deserves a structurally governing status. Appropriateness bears on recognizing the very elements to take into account and the impact of the decision within the causal, logical, and aesthetic context. Such underlying recognitions of importance and appropriateness are necessary and often sufficient conditions of judgment. All the elements are bound together in an interconnected matrix to issue in the form A judges that P.

Whether judgments so cast have truth values has less to do with the fact that they result from the exercise of the judgment than to the theory of truth held. We are here dealing with the truth of P, not "A judges that P." So, estimative judgments that are stand-ins for knowledge when stripped of the prefix "in my judgment" are true or false just as absolute claims of knowledge. Moreover, the truth of such a judgment is close to a conclusive test of its value. On the other hand, a judgment to perform a certain action when recast as, "In circumstances X, A rather than B is the right thing to do," will in a holistic ontology and epistemology also be true or false. Such a view recognizes that at a deep level a seamless web constitutes the world we see, hear, and touch, and the world of thought and value, both aspects of one reality. Indeed, the very pervasiveness of the judgmental function which partakes of both these aspects highlights this interconnectedness. It also suggests that not only are we responsible for our judgments at either end of the spectrum, those that are substantially factual and those that are valuative, but surprisingly we are also intellectually responsible for the vast number of humdrum common sense judgments that fall in between.

As we saw, although cast in the language of fallibility, judgments purport to be correct or true. Thus, because they are distinguished from statements about mere personal liking, preference, or even opinion, there is an implication of a universe of potentially shared judgments which binds us together. Davidson (1984) has pointed out that our language depends upon the largely correct shared view of how things are. At this deep level we must share a view of the same world. I would argue that this conclusion can be widened to constitute a convergence of judgments of right thinking people, which Wittgenstein calls *eine Übereinstimmung in den Urteilen* (1953, no. 242, p. 88e). The circularity is itself specious. In a sense this is reaching Davidson's conclusion of "a shared view of how things are" through the back door, not simply through language but through the implied objectivity of judgments evident in unremarked conduct. Admittedly, this sharing is blurred by the extent to which judgments purport to reflect *how things are* rather than *how they should be* (although even here disagreement is rarer and shallower than commonly supposed). As was said earlier, the degree to which judgments are shared is inversely related to their proximity to values as essential ingredients of those judgments. Such judgments are on the periphery of this shared world, an outer ring of cognitive tolerance, while common sense hugs the center.

While the preceding chapters devoted to clarifying what is meant by the exercise of judgment deserve consideration in their own right, they were also aimed at clearing the conceptual underbrush to permit exploration of the foundational role played by that exercise in the social and intellectual world. To bring that role into the open and try out the concept in the field will be the task of the following pages.

IV

Judgment as Social Function

He that judges without informing himself to the utmost that he
is capable, cannot acquit himself of judging amiss.
> —John Locke, *Essay Concerning
> Human Understanding* II (1690)

Knowledge is the treasure, but judgment the treasurer of a wise
man. He that has more knowledge than judgment is made for
another man's use more than his own.
> —William Penn, *Fruits of Solitude* (1693)

We can think of the world around us, to the extent it is not untouched
nature, as the accretion of millions of judgments made over time,
history's moraine. Here the discussion will be limited to the judgmental function in that part of the residue which comprises our social
institutions. The focus will be on the working of those institutions
that underlie the structure of society: the professions (particularly the
law), politics, and commerce. In these most would agree judgment
plays a considerable role. But there is an inclination to equate judgment to dealing with matters of form rather than substance, to mat-

ters of taste or tact, thereby relegating judgment to the outskirts of what is required to succeed, and allotting primacy to intelligence, knowledge, and hard work. It will be my argument that while these are necessary, they are not, even taken together, sufficient to lead to marked success. In order to appreciate the critical role of judgment I will introduce the concept of *marginal action*. By marginal action I mean *that* action by a professional, politician, businessperson, or individual in the world of affairs which marks the agent as outstanding; in particular, any action significant enough to reflect on the professional quality of the person performing the act. These are the interesting cases to examine. Is there then a faculty or group of faculties that can be isolated as being singularly responsible for the marginal action? If there is, we can call it by analogy the marginal faculty. I will argue that while intelligence, imagination, specialist skill and knowledge are necessary to achieve competence, the *marginal faculty* responsible for marginal actions is judgment.

The Professions

First the professions generally. The centrality of judgment, often hidden with respect to our everyday lives, becomes clearly apparent here. Judgment becomes critical to success. Certain of such judgments depend in large measure on special knowledge and a laboriously acquired skill not available to the layman. But such specialist judgments are entwined with common sense and partake of the same elements. Professional judgments to a greater or lesser degree depend on subsidiary common sense judgments. This is so for several reasons. First, decisions that constitute a professional's practice may be reachable through common sense alone. Second, common-sense decisions are scattered along the way to the narrow professional decision. Third, the ultimate decision reached by a professional requires submission to the test of common sense even though the right professional decision may at times be counterintuitive.

Once it is realized the advice of the professional is not the result of a simple one-dimensional proceeding from A to B to which only the professional has access, there is room for the layperson to question the advice given. There will be links in the judgmental process which will be vulnerable. A single misplaced priority, a single question not asked may invalidate the conclusion. This is particularly true the further we distance ourselves from specialist judgments such as those to determine the dimensions of girders for a bridge or the appropriate material for filling a tooth. The difficulty for the layman lies in discerning these nonspecialist judgmental links hidden in professional decision procedures.

It suggests that the soft professions that have proliferated in the last half century—fields peopled by "how-to" advisers; all manner of designers; and media, financial, and political consultants—should not intimidate us from exercising our own judgment or from questioning theirs. This is so because specialist knowledge is here a relatively minor element forming the judgment in question. With respect to these and indeed all professionals, reliance by the client on the advice given is based largely on trust. Trust in turn is based on reputation which depends on past performance, itself difficult to judge. Success for the client therefore hangs on selection of the right professional, requiring a critical preliminary judgment. Understanding how professional judgments are reached provides a fresh argument for a wide and liberal education. It may not only sharpen our judgmental faculties but provide a factual framework to help us participate in professional decisions that affect us.

So it is elating to realize that the domain open to us is much wider than we supposed. We are not condemned to follow the judgment of professionals without question. The existentialist injunction to create and be responsible for our values can be expanded to areas thought to be inaccessible. But this implies a facility for judging. The question thus arises from the other direction whether the advice of good lawyers and doctors is worth heeding not simply because it is based on specialist knowledge but because the professional is good at judging. Is the person a good lawyer or doctor because she has learned to be a good judge through the practice of her profession or was she a good judge all along which made her a good lawyer or doctor?[50]

---

50. This recalls the coal miner's wistful ditty in *Beyond the Fringe* on the distant joys of judging on the High Court bench.

Lawyers

Law firms traditionally hire candidates based on their marks at law school and what is gleaned from interviews and resumés. They don't have more to go on. The responsible partners observe those hired in drafting pleadings, preparing memoranda of law, settling agreements, analyzing legal rights, and dealing with clients. Degrees of competence begin to emerge. If competence there is adequate, to which performance in the courtroom may later be added, these young lawyers may well remain in the system but without attracting particular note. What will begin to mark them off is how they deal with difficult situations where no ready answer is at hand even to their seniors. Such judgmental elements are present to a lesser or greater degree in all aspects of a lawyer's decision making.

If he is a litigator the dispute comes to the lawyer ready-made and his task is to resolve it, if necessary by assuming the role of advocate in court. The first task is analytic; he must disentangle the issues. To achieve a desired resolution it must be accepted by the other side or, in the absence of settlement, by the court. Litigation is thus a pragmatic exercise that depends on inducing favorable judgments in others. Every step to resolution involves the weighing of competing factors. While the issues are not in themselves linguistic, their resolution often depends on the choice of words. How should the issues be "characterized"? What claims should be put forward? What defenses and counterclaims will they provoke? How should the pleadings be framed? Should extensions of time be requested or granted? When should settlement negotiation be initiated and how conducted? What witnesses to be selected and to what extent coached?

And then the courtroom tactics. What evidence to lead, what questions to avoid or ask, and how to ask them? What arguments to deploy to counter the judge's concerns? How to press a point? How to lay the groundwork for an appeal? In all this, issues relating to determining the general law may play a minor role and confrontations will be narrowed to its particular application. The result may turn on can the case at hand be distinguished from the precedents that constitute the cited law? But even here the emphasis lies with the facts, with convincing the court to characterize them in a certain way. It comes as a mild surprise to the graduate emerging from law school that mastering the facts is the secret to courtroom success. That is so not only because most trials are simply about establishing the facts but because determining the applicable law to the case at hand is itself shaped by the way those facts are put.

In all litigation there is inherent uncertainty as to the result; therefore the critical role of prediction at every stage of the process. In our adversarial system, because of different inputs as to the factual content provided by their respective clients and different judgments as to how the law will be applied with respect to those inputs, counsel on opposite sides arrive at different predictions as to the result. Cases are settled before trial to the extent that the range of predictive judgments overlap. The recalcitrant cases that survive for trial are those in which such judgments don't. So the litigator's ability to predict the consequences of his every act to the conclusion of the trial, subject to constant revision, is critical to success. Such predictions will determine his judgment on the advisability of settlement. Finally, the courtroom lawyer is acutely aware of the constant balancing required between his duty to his client, the court, and the ethics of the profession. Judgment is central to advocacy.

The role of the commercial lawyer requires judgmental faculties of a different order. His client approaches him with a commercial project. It is for the commercial lawyer to find the legal means to put it into effect. Western systems of commercial law contain within themselves an empty domain circumscribed by certain overriding rules (the law of contract) which permit its occupation by a private body of rules, created by and between commercial entities, that will be recognized and enforced by the courts. This opportunity calls for a highly creative turn of mind in the commercial lawyer that will suggest to the parties structures to accommodate their respective commercial objectives.

The enterprise of constructing a private legal system within the broader public legal one is therefore essentially synthetic. The judgmental elements are prominent throughout. There is the ongoing interaction with the client. To what extent is it appropriate to probe the clarity of the client's intent? What are her priorities in the negotiations to follow? Will the client's or lawyer's insistence on a point provoke the other side to walk away? When is due diligence satisfied? What are the client's implicit factual assumptions that must be made explicit in the documentation? What is the appropriate level of representations and covenants to be demanded? To what extent should the lawyer simply rely on instructions and repress his own concerns; to what extent should his lay knowledge and common sense intrude into the business decision? There is the appropriateness of the form of contract. How far to tilt the first draft in favor of the client within the limits of reality and fairness? How much formality? What may appear form to one may be substance to the other.

By his structural sense of what are the key business issues, the lawyer ensures that the right questions have been asked. But the best lawyer will stretch his imagination to conjure up alternate structures that may better satisfy the client's needs, and with it the world of alternate implied consequences to be guarded against. All this will register on his mental computer screen as a constant reordering of negotiating priorities. Although lawyers are fond of demarcating business from legal issues, drawing that convenient line is itself judgmental. It may be appropriate to advise the client of the lawyer's own views if he sees the transaction going off the rails. Yet the lawyer must know when to pull back and let the client decide. He will exercise the skill peculiar to a commercial practitioner to bridge differences between the parties by verbal formulae that will accommodate both.

If the structure of the law is well embedded, feeling the latest winkles at the fingertips is not critical. These must in any event be run down before final advice is given. What is more important is to grasp the shape of the issues, characterize them, and place them in the context of the client's needs, all judgmental functions. Where rules, procedures, or considerations conflict, the lawyer must have a sure feel for the central. What he must also know is what is *not* an issue, what is merely legalistic, what is *de minimis,* when to go by the book, and when not.

While the lawyer will have in mind certain nonlegal lateral implications and commercial consequences of proposed provisions, the judgmental challenge is to fix how far his obligation extends. Once suggested, such implications and consequences may be provided for. But whose job is it to summon them up? How far foresight? What haunts the practitioner putting a deal together, apart from any legal obligation, is the uncertainty of the extent of his responsibility for the transaction. Will it work? For, many of the concepts, indeed the structure of the deal itself, are fashioned by an interplay between lawyer and client. Hence judgment has a creative role in concept formation. And in difficult negotiations the most taxing case may be the unheeding client. So companies have been lost while their advisers stood by helplessly. Or did they?

Time is inevitably of the essence at the closing of a transaction. Every word in the formal opinion to be delivered requires a judgment as to form and substance, although probably not a fresh one. The route is often hazardous, requiring subsidiary judgments; sometimes it allows shades and subtleties, at others no qualification or temporizing. Apart from the opinion, the agenda for closing calls for the delivery of dozens if not hundreds of other documents. Inevitably, one or more aren't. What to do? The client looks to his lawyer for advice on whether to give on the point. Is the disputed issue or the missing document critical? Can the additional risk be isolated, quantified, and assumed? Does the client really understand the risk? The transaction and its consequences may hang on the judgment. At rare moments, closings (usually through a change of circumstance) approach high drama where the pressure to make judgments that may lead to litigation is intense.

Usage and convention provide answers to many of these questions. And much can be learned from observing senior practitioners. But experience can be no infallible guide to what is inevitably a judgment made on the spot by one's best lights. Having the appropriate degree of confidence in one's own judgment is itself essential. Often the lawyer takes refuge by seeking instructions from the client but the lawyer must know when this is a proper shift of the burden. The centrality of judgment is compounded by the advice sought on how clients should exercise theirs, advice cautiously given by indirection on what matters to take into account. Ultimately the lawyer must look to the guides of importance and appropriateness. How he follows them to arrive at a judgment lies deep within him.

So a lawyer's day is a continuum of judgments. It is not the lawyer's intelligence or knowledge that marks off the conspicuous performer. It is judgments exercised in the boardroom, the courtroom, and in the privacy of the office that distinguish his marginal actions.[51] And what is clearer still at the other extreme is that bad judgment may end a career.

---

51. A bold recognition by the legal academy of the centrality of imagination and judgment to the legal profession is given by Vincent Blasi in his remarks to the 1993 class of Columbia Law School (printed in 1993–1994 prospectus for Columbia University's Juris Doctor program):

I think there are 25 law schools in the country where the analytical rigor with which law is taught is comparable to Columbia's high standards. Again, that is not a reason to come to Columbia. The reason to come to Columbia has to do with two other elements crucial to a legal education. One is imagination and the other is judgment.

Imagination. What really separates a great lawyer from a good one, I believe, is the ability to think originally, albeit within a discipline, using a common core of information and common analytical techniques. To think originally as a lawyer is to see distinctions and connections, premises and consequences, problems and possibilities that other people have not previously noticed. . . .

Judgment. This is something that has no real sex appeal. It is not glorified when people think about what makes an outstanding law student or an outstanding lawyer. But, if I ask myself whom would I really want as my lawyer, or whom do I really want deciding an important issue of public policy, I think good judgment matters more than brilliance or encyclopedic knowledge. Well, how do you develop good judgment? We can't teach you good judgment. Maybe we can provide examples.

Courts

Discussion of lawyers leads naturally to what is considered the paradigm of judgment, one that is delivered by a court. Note first that there are apparent anomalies in considering what judges and juries do in courtrooms. We have said that simply reading off features from a scale or arriving at results under optimum conditions (where we have the right to expect the right answer) is not exercising judgment. Yet the laws are a set of rules that purport to function like a scale. If laws were clear, unambiguous, and part of a closed system like arithmetic (*pace* Gödel), their application would paradoxically not constitute judgment. But laws are in the main open-textured (to use H. L. A. Hart's term), that is, formally imperfect and subject to extension and contraction. A court's judgment consists in construing the rule and applying it to the case at hand. The effect may expand or contract the scope of the rule as a result of a complex process.

First the judge must make judgments (findings) of fact which in turn depend on judgments of credibility,[52] sometimes made by a jury—Locke's conjoining of ideas.[53] Then the judge must carry out

---

52. The Cretan liar paradox came to life in the review by the Supreme Court of Canada of the murder conviction of David Milgaard twenty-one years earlier based largely on the evidence of one Wilson. Wilson was called by Milgaard's lawyer to testify before the Supreme Court that the evidence he gave at the trial was false, which he did. But during the course of his new evidence the Supreme Court found he was lying. The Chief Justice, in citing Wilson for contempt, said, "You lied to us yesterday and you lied to us in your recanting." (*The Globe and Mail,* January 24, 1992)

53. That the question of credibility is ultimately the sole responsibility of the trier of fact (whether judge or jury) was brought home by a 1993 decision of the Supreme Court of Canada (*Marquard* v *H.M. the Queen*) in which the issue was the credibility of a three-and-a-half-year-old girl testifying on an alleged assault by her grandmother. The court drew a fine but clear line between admissible expert evidence on psychological factors that may lead to certain behavior relevant to credibility in general and inadmissible expert evidence on the credibility of a particular witness. Justice McLachlin, speaking for the majority, said,

a complex process of *applying* the law to the facts as she sees them. The tests of importance and appropriateness operating through the concepts of relevance, weight, and equity are much in evidence. We have seen that applying a rule is itself a mysterious process with respect to which there are no further rules to appeal to. So where in a clear-cut criminal case all the ingredients of the crime are proved beyond a reasonable doubt, there may be very little judgment involved with respect to the application of an established rule.

On the other hand, in civil cases unpredictability of the result is systemic. If the parties and their counsel were reasonably certain of the same result, they would not be in court. The weekly law reports are wonderfully full of surprises. It is the very uncertainty of the application of the law to specific circumstances (or to the findings of fact) that drives litigation. I call this the *paradox of predictability*. The paradox lies in the juxtaposition of this systematic unpredictability with respect to specific decisions and our assumption that the law has high predictive power in order to regulate conduct. What meaning can be given to predictability when opposing professionals as a matter of course predict or countenance opposing results? As I put it elsewhere:

> Litigation represents in effect the flip side of the law—the recalcitrant instances where the law has failed to convince. It is a paradox to have a profession and social institution trade on the systematic unpredictability of specific applications of the law that in general must be assumed to be predictable in prin-

---

It is a fundamental axiom of our trial process that the ultimate conclusion as to the credibility or truthfulness of a particular witness is for the trier of fact, and is not the proper subject of expert opinion. . . . A judge or jury who simply accepts an expert's opinion on the credibility of a witness would be abandoning its duty to itself [to] determine the credibility of the witness. Credibility must always be the product of the judge or jury's view of the diverse ingredients it has perceived at trial, combined with experience, logic, and an intuitive sense of the matter . . . there is a growing consensus that while expert evidence on the ultimate credibility of a witness is not admissible, expert evidence on human conduct and the psychological and physical factors which may lead to certain behavior relevant to credibility, is admissible.

ciple in order to qualify as a system of rules. It is a paradox that the law is by and large predictable but particular judicial decisions are not. Perhaps in recognition of this paradox, counsel do not tell their clients what the law is, they give opinions. And when the decision in court goes against them, counsel cannot be sued on those opinions unless they are made negligently.[54]

The image is of a trickle of water starting along a dry pavement. One may be able to predict the general direction but not the next squiggle. But it is only the next squiggle that concerns the litigant.[55]

---

54. In this discussion I draw heavily on my article "Dworkin's Empire and What Goes on in the Courtroom" (1989). I there argue that Ronald Dworkin together with many legal academics is mistaken in attempting to understand what takes place in the courtroom on the basis of disagreement between lawyers:

He follows other legal philosophers in assuming that disagreement among lawyers is a matter of conflicting belief. . . . Does disagreement among lawyers require psychological commitment, that is belief, or simply an inconsistency in the statements made? In truth if we look at the actual practice of lawyers, we seldom find disagreement in belief about what the law *is*. . . . Indeed, in our legal tradition it is improper for counsel to state what counsel *believes* the law to be. . . . Counsel makes a *submission* and urges the court to adopt it, giving reasons that he/she considers persuasive. . . . We should regard disagreement of counsel in adversarial systems of law as *sui generis*.

But what about judges? There is often disagreement between an appellate court and a court below and among judges of an appellate court. Our judicial system demands of judges a critical upward shift in the belief content of any statement of the law. While judges believe what they say about the law, what counts as a primary social fact is their finding for or against the parties. The disagreements between courts and among judges are, therefore, in the first (and last) instance, disagreements as to result.

55. The thesis that there are always recognizable principles that underlie judicial decisions is given a certain intuitive plausibility when examples are drawn from criminal law or constitutional law where the conflicting rights of the parties fairly shine through the pages ready to be acknowledged by the courts. It is noteworthy that examples from commercial law are rarely mentioned by legal philosophers even though such

cases by their starkness in terms of "values" should test any jurisprudential theory. The troubling cases in contract and in tort are those where the conflict is between innocent parties stranded by a wrongdoer. Take for example the decision of the British Columbia Court of Appeal in *National Trust Company Limited* v *Bank of Montreal et al.* (1985 DLR[4]22). This was a dispute between two creditors of a real estate developer as to their respective rights to $38 million of marketable securities. The issue turned on whether a prohibition against long-term debt and security in a trust deed in favor of one creditor was breached by a later security granted the other. That issue in turn depended on whether four discrete, almost identical securities each limited to the permitted period given back-to-back on their expiry should be deemed one security that infringed the duration prohibition. The majority found a breach of the prior security, giving weight to intention and the overall effect of the transaction. The dissenting judge gave primary weight to the documentation on the view that in a technical matter such as this, form *is* substance and intent and effect are irrelevant. One might ask whether compliance with form is not here a higher, relevant level of intent applicable particularly to commercial transactions to stiffen the law's backbone of predictability.

The issue of form and substance, parts and the whole, had a different twist in another case I had a part in some twenty-five years earlier (*Stratton Estate* v *Trans Canada Air Lines,* 1961 WWR 183). The case arose out of the crash of a TCA plane on a flight from Vancouver to Calgary. The issue was whether the provisions of the Warsaw Convention enacted into Canadian law applied to limit severely the damages payable by TCA to the estate of the deceased. That in turn depended on whether the Vancouver-Calgary flight was deemed part of an international flight with respect to that passenger. Under the Convention a series of separate flights, possibly entirely domestic, possibly with different carriers, are deemed one international flight ("carriage") if even one leg has a destination in another country and if the series of flights has been regarded as a single operation by the parties. The deceased had purchased a ticket in Los Angeles to fly to Seattle and then on to Victoria, B.C., from where he was to fly to Vancouver, all segments of which were clearly parts of one international flight. But on arrival in Seattle the passenger decided to fly to Vancouver directly and then on to Calgary by connecting flight and made the necessary reservation. However, he was advised to buy the Vancouver-Calgary portion of the ticket in Vancouver to save U.S. tax. The judge, upheld on appeal, found that the ill-fated flight to Calgary was not part of the international flight and thus the Convention limiting liability did not apply. One could say that in *Stratton,* form triumphs over the intent of the legislation, although even this ratio is dubious. In both cases there was little precedent to follow, no obvious principles, simply differing reasons advanced by both sides leading to an unpredictable judgment "on the facts."

There is no exhaustive list of considerations to which the judge consciously or unconsciously appeals to render the main and subsidiary judgments that lead to (or back from) the final decision. Judges are appointed not simply because they are thought to know the law but because they are considered to be good at exercising judgment, and where appropriate, articulating the path. Their job is that exercise. Uncertainty is reduced by providing rules of process and considerations that are appropriate or inappropriate in forming the judgment. These themselves may be the subject of further judgment. Every court's judgment has a double function: it not only disposes of the particular matter before it, but, simply by virtue of being made, declares the law on the point. Whether it declares rightly or wrongly will only be determined by other later judgments. The safety net provided by civilized legal systems gives an opening for another set of judges to substitute their judgment for the judgment appealed from. This provides a further chance for intersubjective triangulation (Davidson's phrase) to work toward the right decision.

I now want to relate what has been said in the previous chapter about the application of rules more particularly to the process of adjudication. All rules imply the possibility of their application and the paradox of predictability springs from the distinction between a rule at time t_1 and how that rule will be applied at time t_2. It is the legislative function to create and define the rule in terms of varying specificity; it is the judicial function to determine whether and how such rule applies in particular instances. Well-formed rules assume that logical derivation will determine the application of the rule to a specific instance. Application in this narrow sense applies to a law of the form, *if A then B*, by the judge determining that as A exists (or X exists and X is an A) therefore B. If the application of law were confined to this deductive procedure, then at any rate if the parties agree that A exists, the rest could safely be left to a computer.

But because laws in a legal system describe the circumstances of their application in degrees of generality and the members of the set A (or B) are not exhaustively defined, or capable by identification in advance, mere logical derivation becomes inadequate and application of the law, that is adjudication, becomes parasitic on legislation. The convenient distinction between legislative and judicial functions becomes clouded. Say that the judge determines that *A* should include reference to circumstances described as (*a*) and that the consequences are not simply *B* but also (*b*). Then the result of a judge's application of the law becomes, *if A* + (*a*) then *B* + (*b*). Or, alternatively, she may decide in the presence of (*a*) that *B* will not follow. In either such case, her decision will constitute an elaboration of the original law and will to that extent constitute legislation. And this is so even in statute-centered systems and in those jurisdictions that do not have a strict doctrine of precedent.[56]

The central concept to examine in adjudication is therefore not the interpretation of the law but its application. In commonsense terms interpretation is a prior function to application. It makes sense to say that we understand (that we have *interpreted* in the everyday sense) a rule even if we cannot predict all the instances of its application. Understood social rules retain a residue of generality that requires a further decision on how to apply them in a particular case. Whether to apply a rule ultimately depends on those ill-understood criteria such as importance and appropriateness that were discussed earlier, that is, the elements of judgment. The "hard cases" of legal writers are simply a refined special case of what confronts us daily.

So the act of application of the law is pushed back to an act of judgment. That is another way of saying that there is no rule to tell us how to apply a rule. Kant pointed out that to posit rules to apply rules would lead to an infinite regress. It makes sense to question judgments and any of the ingredients or reasons given for them. But ultimately one judgment can only be replaced by another judgment, one human decision for another. At this point

---

56. Aristotle puts it thus: "So when the law states a general rule, and a case arises under this that is exceptional, then it is right, where the legislator owing to the generality of his language has erred in not covering that case, to correct the omission by a ruling such as the legislator himself would have given if he had been present there, and as he would have enacted if he had been aware of the circumstances" (*Ethics* V.x.1137b).

one can go no further.[57] When Justice Harry Blackmun was asked how he reached decisions in the United States Supreme Court involving difficult social or constitutional issues he replied, "It just comes from one's exercise as best (one) can, of the judgment (one) possesses."[58] That is what judges are appointed to do.[59] Appeal must be made to factors outside a system which cannot be self-contained. Laurence Tribe observes (1992):

> The great philosopher and mathematician Kurt Gödel in fact proved decades ago that no logical or linguistic system rich enough to permit elementary arithmetic functions can be completely self-contained. Indeed, our Constitution's Ninth Amendment expressly acknowledges that "the People"—perhaps as individuals, perhaps as a collectivity—retain "rights" not "enumerated" in the document itself.

It may be thought that the appeal to these external factors that are ingredients in judicial discretion provides the judge with justi-

---

57. But see Gadamer, who appears to avoid the issue by pushing the process back to a "better law," i.e., equity:

> The situation of the person "applying" law is quite different. In a certain instance he will have to refrain from applying the full rigor of the law. But if he does, it is not because he has no alternative, but because to do otherwise would not be right. In restraining the law, he is not diminishing it but, on the contrary, finding the better law. Aristotle expresses this very clearly in his analysis of epieikeia (equity): epieikeia is the correction of the law. (1992, 318)

58. Interview with Bill Moyers, PBS, April 16, 1987.

59. Anthony Lewis, as quoted by Peter Steinberger (1993, 1), commenting on the controversy over Robert Bork's nomination to the United States Supreme Court in the *New York Times,* September 27, 1987, writes:

> Judge Bork's extraordinary five days of testimony left the senators with a task that [Former Attorney General] Katzenbach stated sensitively. "Were I in your position," he told the committee, "the central question I would be asking is this. Is Judge Bork a man of judgment? Not intellect, not reasoning, not lawyering skills, not ideology, not philosophy—simply judgment. Is he a wise person?"

fication for subjective considerations. But such discretion, reserved for limited circumstances such as custody applications, is simply a special case of getting a particular decision right. Justice McLachlin of the Supreme Court of Canada has said that judicial discretion "is a very special thing . . . an exercise in objectivity. . . . In other words, the judge is not simply imposing his or her cultural views, or lifestyle views, or values in making a custody decision" (as quoted in *The Lawyers Weekly,* December 10, 1993).[60]

Beyond judicial discretion there is the consideration of justice. While the concept of justice itself may be abstract and general, yet doing justice, sought at the Lord Chancellor's foot, necessarily inheres in the particular—the act, the parties and the circumstances.[61]

How does this way of looking at the judicial process affect the court's role in the debate on collective and community rights? There are two issues here often run together. First, what is the content of such rights? Second, should the content be determined on the political level or at the judicial level on the basis of inherent or constitutional rights? Clearly the action has moved to the courts. So collectives can obtain wholesale relief from courts without the pain of political bargaining. In this shift from the political to the legal, gross wrongs are sometimes righted but at a procedural and substantive cost: procedural because the effect is legislative, substantive because judicially packaged rights may deny or distort other social ideals.[62] The procedural danger posed,

----

60. Notwithstanding this avowal, there is concern in the cries for a more "representative" judiciary that judges will cross the line from heightened objectivity discussed earlier to the championing of the represented group's interest inconsistent with impartiality, a derivative of objectivity.

61. This account of the judicial decision is not incompatible with Richard Wasserstrom's (1961) two-level procedure of justification in which the judge seeks first to frame a law or rule to cover the decision, and then seeks adequate reasons to justify the law or rule. However, while it is a tautology that rules and laws must play and appear to play a central role in the law, their proper place in judicial decision making is more oblique than Wasserstrom suggests.

62. The judicial tide appears to be turning on gerrymandering to further minority representation. The 1993 U.S. Supreme Court decision in *Shaw* v *Reno* (125 L Ed 2d 511) ruled that redistricting a North Carolina

common to constitutional issues, is the absence of safeguards provided by the court's traditional function of judging narrow issues
where the shadow cast is short. But pronouncing rights to token
litigants of collectives may darken a distant landscape, once the
individual *qua* individual is abandoned as the elemental particle in
the judicial system of a given society. After all, with a little effort
legitimate "collective rights" can be derived from traditional individual rights to equality, nondiscrimination, and so on. Once
inherent rights are accorded to subgroups as ultimate and not
derivative from paramount individual rights, the civil protections
gained since the seventeenth century will be eroded. It is the proper business of the *political* process as reflected in legislation to
define rights of subgroups within a society.[63]

How this bears on judgment should be clear. Rights are halfway houses that become unsafe when judgment as to their specific application cannot be foreseen. A safer, more legitimate
haven is provided by the political process that must negotiate
between competing ideals to arrive at the right solution to a par-

---

congressional district for the purpose of ensuring the election of one racial
group reinforces impermissible racial stereotypes, namely that members of
a minority "think alike, share the same political interests and will prefer
the same candidates at the polls." Justice O'Connor speaking for the
majority continued, "The message that such districting sends to elected
representatives is equally pernicious. When a district obviously is created
solely to effectuate the perceived common interests of one racial group,
elected officials are more likely to believe that their primary obligation is
to represent only the member of that group, rather than the constituency as
a whole. This is altogether antithetical to our system of representative
democracy." The fine judgmental line is indicated in the dissenting judgment of Justice Souter who points out that it is a well-established rule in
redistricting that "some considerations of race for legitimate reasons" can
be taken into account.

63. The case of aboriginal people is not so much a historical exception as a confirmation. For their case for collective rights is most persuasive when based on their claim as a *separate* society and most workable
when coupled with territorial separation. *Within* the society many of their
claims need be heeded as those of other sufferers, not on ethnic but on
political and moral grounds.

ticular complex issue.[64] And in the resulting legislation there will be reference simply to states of affairs and mention of "rights" will fall by the wayside.[65] Albeit, the legislation, no matter how narrowly drafted, will itself require not only particularization by the courts, but also prioritization, particularly where constitutional rights are in question.

Here it is important to note that typically, constitutional rights are simply listed and not prioritized. It would be impossible for the drafters to pick priorities among principles, all of which are seen as fundamental. Of course, constitutions may, as in the "Charter" provisions of the Canadian constitution, contain exceptions to paramount principles explicitly, or by shifting the onus of proof. But that simply lets in another fundamental principle to push the decision process one step farther back. Thus, to avoid conflict there must be an appeal to the concepts of importance and centrality as they bear on a particular case. Take the case of a publication ban by a trial judge on the proceedings of one criminal trial in order to ensure a fair later trial of a co-accused. Here the rights of free speech and the press come up against the rights

---

64. John Gray arrives at the same position by a different route:

The discourse of rights increasingly drives out all others from political life. If the theoretical goal of the new liberalism is the supplanting of politics by law, its practical result—especially in America, where rights discourse is already the only public discourse that retains any legitimacy—has been the emptying of political life of substantive argument and the political corruption of law. Issues, such as abortion, that in many other countries have been resolved by a legislative settlement that involves compromise and which is known to be politically negotiable, are in the United States matters of fundamental rights that are intractably contested and which threaten to become enemies of civil peace.

(*Times Literary Supplement*, July 3, 1992)

A similar view was elaborated by Jean Elshtain (1993) in her CBC Massey Lectures, "Democracy on Trial."

65. Much as the troublesome terms "meaning" and "interpretation" drop out where communication is successful, as discussed under "Cognition" in the last chapter.

to a fair trial which in turn may affect the life and liberty of the individual.[66] So considerations of importance and centrality on the priority of specific constitutional rights in the particular circumstances will determine the issue.

After this excursion we have come back to the act of judgment to determine the particular. Which leads to what is for jurisprudence a rather extreme view, that the area entered by the cutting edge of the law is not only systematically unmapped but unmappable. Here "cutting edge" carries both meanings, the business-end of the process and the frontier. The judge's real work begins at the border where the clear application of a rule gives out, where the given law comes to an end. We need open our eyes and see the emperor only half clothed, as every litigator does when he climbs the courthouse steps uncertain what the day will bring.

Thus the majesty of the law lies less in the principles laid down by Lords Mansfield, Atkin, and Denning or Justices Holmes and Cardozo, but rather in the countless Solomonic judgments handed down by trial judges disentangling the web of argument and evidence before them into single judgments that are so often seen as right. It is a marvel that society in the main is content to repose its trust in these solitary decisions.

---

66. See the Supreme Court of Canada decision *Dagenais* v *Canadian Broadcasting Corporation* (1994 S.C.C. preliminary report, p. 33) where the majority of the court deciding against the legality of a publication ban ruled per Chief Justice Lamer:

> When the protected rights of two individuals come into conflict, as can occur in the case of publication bans, Charter principles require a balance to be achieved that fully respects the *importance* of both sets of rights.
> A publication ban should only be ordered when:
> (a) Such a ban is necessary in order to prevent a *real* and *substantial* risk to the fairness of the trial, because reasonably available alternative measures will not prevent the risk; and
> (b) The salutary effects of the publication ban *outweigh* the deleterious effects to the free expression of those affected by the ban.
> [Emphasis mine]

Thus, not unexpectedly, appeal is left to concepts of importance and weight.

Other Professions

What has been said about the centrality of judgment with respect to the law is true only to a somewhat lesser degree with respect to the other professions. In medicine it is critical to diagnosis and prescription. There are vital attitudinal and ethical issues. How to balance the benefits and risks of new drugs, techniques, and therapies? Here the judgmental factors are clear. The recent movement in medicine to induce patients to take a measure of responsibility for their treatment springs from a recognition that often the appropriate judgment depends on the correct reading of an indefinite number of variables that can only be fully known by the patient. The physician informs the patient of the alternatives that lead to a joint judgment on the appropriate diagnosis and prescription.

While the central role of judgment in law and medicine is transparent, its presence in the number-crunching professions of accounting and engineering is submerged. We look to accountants to deliver the kind of certainty paralleled by mathematics in the intellectual realm. After all, the bottom line of a commercial enterprise is the basis of business decisions.[67]

Yet the calculation of profits and assets is rife with judgmental components. The tip-off is in the auditor's imprimatur that the financial statements in the auditor's opinion reflect *fairly* (note, not simply accurately or not just even truthfully) the financial position of the audited company. There is thus an implicit disclaimer signalled by the reference to the concept *fair.* This brings in the judgment of what is material. Next in generality is the underlying rule of generally accepted accounting principles (GAAP), which vary somewhat by jurisdiction, including the rule that financial statements be on an accrual rather than on a cash basis, common also to most tax systems. The spate of one-time charges in reported financial results signals built-up discrepancies or new rules that testify to judgmental shifts. The con-

---

67. Note the movement to "multiple bottom lines" to record progress to social and environmental, and not just financial goals.

cept of *fiscal period* entails cutting off the ongoing operation being audited into defined time segments and exercising judgment as to which period assets and liabilities should be allocated. The distinction between capital and income critical to GAAP and to taxation requires further judgmental determinations between capitalizing expenses such as interest and research, or treating them as ingredients in the determination of income.

The goal of fairness, that is the attempt to reflect the "real" state of a company's present financial condition, implies reaching into the past and stretching into the future. As assets and liabilities are stated at historic cost subject only to arbitrary rates of depreciation, the issue remains whether assets should be revalued upward and liabilities downward to account for inflation or, in theory, vice versa in deflation. The goal also underlies the attempt to quantify the present risk of future liabilities. Thus the difficulty of determining the amount of reserves to be provided for such traditional categories as doubtful receivables or depreciation of capital assets. But beyond determining the amount of a reserve the broader judgmental issue is what future risks are to be reserved against. The list is ever-growing. Reserves are now required for future capital expenditures that may be required by environmental regulations and future tax increases. Hence, as all assets and liabilities have a forward aspect to them, one can quite "reserve away" the present into the future. Given that the present is different from the future and the goal of financial statements is to give a fair picture of the present, doesn't the concept of notional reserves become self-defeating?

Regulatory bodies such as the professional governing societies and the Financial Accounting Standards Board in the United States have set out rules and guidelines on such matters, although which to regulate is itself a judgmental issue. Their application will also depend on judgment in the individual instance. Experience has shown that the treatment by different accountants in seemingly similar circumstances can differ widely, as has the evidence in court. The Institute of Chartered Accountants of Alberta, commenting on the 1989 inquiry into the failure of two Alberta banks, said:

The opinions of Mr. Justice Estey relate to issues of *audit judgment*. It is the task of the auditor to obtain sufficient *appropriate* evidence to support an opinion as to whether financial statements prepared by corporation's management and approved by its board of directors fairly present the corporation's financial position. [Emphasis mine]

In addition to the judgmental factors involved in the determination of specific ingredients in an audit, judgment in a more general sense enters into determinations made by accountants. Thus, in judgments as to the estimated profitability of a contemplated acquisition, should the appropriate test be the *marginal* increased costs and revenue or such factors calculated on a *cost accounting* basis allocated over the whole business? The answers will vary markedly and thus perhaps the client's decision on the transaction.

Another number-dominated profession, engineering, does not escape the demands of judgment. This becomes apparent in liability actions against engineers relating to the collapse of roofs, bridges, and other structures where professional judgment is the issue. Take the case of a structural engineer designing an earthquake-proof building. He must determine the seismic horizontal loads that will be imposed on the structure by pressures in the surrounding earth. These will be determined in a highly complex way by the design of the structure. Pressures on the building in turn will be determined by the design of the building. For example, whether its surface is considered one "wall" or several walls separated by windows, will affect the calculation in different ways. Again, the ability of the building to withstand shocks will be determined by its height from the *ground,* and the structure below. Yet there has been argument over what constitutes "the ground." While there are accepted rules, the answer is site specific.

Or take the case of a geotechnical engineer conducting a subsurface investigation. There are frequent disputes as to the frequency and the pattern of holes that should be drilled in order to determine the substructure. The transcripts of court proceedings are replete with evidence of expert witnesses whose testimony runs "in my professional judgment, in these circumstances. . . ."

The same considerations are true of architecture to the extent the profession partakes of engineering. To the extent an architect's function is aesthetic, the place of judgment is obvious as is the resolution of the occasional dilemma between the architect's aesthetic position and the needs or wishes of the client.

There are the less academic professions. There is the field commander for whom tactics and strategy must be adapted to meet the changing situation at hand. There is the discretion required of those responsible for law enforcement which determines a society's civility. There is the choice by a newspaper editor as to which story to run and the appropriate headline, which in turn affects countless other judgments. There is the urban planner and the examples of enlightened citizens attempting to undo misjudgments on the building of freeways and ghettos. There is the banker and broker admonished to know their clients. But how far? There are parole boards on whose judgments lives may hang.

Finally, judgment plays the central role in what is perhaps the most important profession of all, teaching (unless we count parenting). Judgment on how to present material, how to conduct a class, and what image to present is required even in the inspired teacher.

Kant understood the plight of professionals:

> A physician, a judge, or a ruler may have at command many excellent pathological, legal, or political rules, even to the degree that he may become a profound teacher of them, and yet, nonetheless, may easily stumble in their application. For, although admirable in understanding, he may be wanting in natural power of judgment. He may comprehend the universal *in abstracto,* and yet not be able to distinguish whether a case *in concreto* comes under it.
>
> (Kant 1985, 178)

The exercise of judgment in particular circumstances is therefore a defining quality of professionalism. There are of course others, of which the utter commitment to the Work and its quality in and for itself is perhaps paramount. But without the capacity for judgment there is no hope of discharging such commitment. At times "God (or the devil) is in the details," at others a Flemish fascination with the minute obscures the outline of the structure. We look to a professional not only for knowledge of the rules but also for the judgment to apply them (or not) where the signposts point different ways. Sometimes we look there to our loss. For as we saw, the judgments of editors, lawyers, and all manner of advisors have a cascading effect on the judgments of others, compounding what went right or wrong.

It is the professional's ability to perform in these sorts of cases that wins our respect. And it is inconceivable that someone who has reached the top would be thought to have poor judgment. Professionalism lies in means, the *appropriate* modulation of means to reach a result. Means also implies *manner.* The common word recalls something seemingly quite unrelated, the motto of the fifteenth-century Bishop of Waynflete, "Manners Makyth Man." The phrase reminds us that how we conduct ourselves and how we achieve our external objectives are both dependent on the choice of means which in turn defines us.[68]

Politics

It is well known that a disproportionately large number of politicians start as lawyers. This has been variously attributed to their independent economic circumstances, their facility with manipulating language, and their day-to-day exposure to laws which are the end product of politics. But there is an even stronger connection. It is that the lawyer's preoccupation with exercising judgment leads more easily than others to what is at the heart of politics. For in politics even more than in law, judgment, as Aristotle noted, is the paramount skill.

In a democracy a politician must first get and stay elected.

---

68. Stanley Cavell (1990, 127) paraphrases Emerson's lesson in "Manners": "[M]anners are more important to humankind than we imagine and less important than we think." There is also Edmund Burke's "Manners are of more importance than laws. Upon them in a great measure, the laws depend" (*Letters on a Regicide Peace,* 1797).

Alliances must be forged, lobbies appeased. The enactment of legislation is itself also a matter of compromise. It is not cynicism to suggest that even at the loftiest level the statesman in making judgments on the content, form, and timing of policy keeps in mind their effect on his political capital. Because it cannot follow a predetermined agenda, Western liberalism for the generation of policy is particularly susceptible to the continuous exercise of judgment on an *ad hoc* basis.[69] For a liberal what is politically correct probably isn't. It is not a cliché to think of liberalism as a state of mind, for which agendas are an ever-present danger. A liberal wishes to right wrongs without creating new ones.[70] Sometimes that may mean abstaining from causes. Hence the dilemma of party platforms. Judgment is the mechanism with which the liberal mind by appeal to a handful of ideals molds strategies to fit the irregular shifting contours of the world. The spirit of the age gives to these lodestars its own voice: authenticity, autonomy, civility, and the familiar survivor, *fairness*.[71]

It is the genius of the English-speaking world to have articulated a concept that appears to run in a more diffuse way elsewhere. John Rawls (1972) appeals to this intuitive concept of fairness in his explication of justice. Indeed, it is difficult to go much beyond that feeling except to note that its content is always

---

69. When combined with a required prudence, judgment leads to "the first rule of politics is not to deal with hypothetical situations" (Perrin Beatty, Canada's then Minister of Communications, as reported in the *Globe and Mail,* August 29, 1992).

70. The dangers of "principle" were discussed earlier. It is trenchantly put by Isaiah Berlin in his article on Alexander Herzen (*Encounter,* May 1956): "The thesis which Herzen offered to the world comes to this: that any attempt to explain human conduct in terms of, or to dedicate human beings to the service of, any abstraction, be it never so noble—justice, progress, nationality—even if preached by impeccable altruists like Mazzini or Louis Blanc or Mill, always leads in the end to victimization and human sacrifice."

71. Richard Rorty goes further and maintains (*Times Literary Supplement,* June 1994) that there is no theory of political philosophy that can justify liberal democracy. One can only give good reasons for specific measures.

driven by particular facts. Judgment as to what is thus required for fairness, what is important and appropriate in the circumstances, cannot be abdicated by a subscription to what is politically correct.[72]

Equity, which overlaps fairness, purports to play a central role in the formulation of social policy. As with fairness, the challenge is to apply the concept to the particular case. I examined the problems inherent in such applications in an article on the formulation of taxation policy. I argued there, anticipating Rawls, that an equitable tax system must not be inconsistent with predictions as to its effect on the actual welfare of the poorest class. So a policy of soaking the rich is not *ipso facto* equitable:

> If equity were at stake it would be hard to argue that in case of conflict the policy which advanced the welfare of the poor the most should not deserve priority. Nor would the poor listen.
>
> (1968, 471)

Thomas Sowell traces the difficulty of determining equity to the mistaken notion that

> goods and services have some "real," "true," or "just" value, which third parties can determine. The doctrine of "comparable worth" is the clearest contemporary expression of this medieval fallacy. . . . The very fact that economic transactions take place shows that there is no objective "real" value. The seller sells because he values what he gets more than he values what he gives up. But the buyer buys for exactly the same rea-

---

72. Fairness and appropriateness are themselves intertwined. Formerly it had been thought appropriate that certain perquisites and privileges attach to membership in Parliament or the Congress. Thus, fairness did not arise. Such perquisites and privileges not available to all are now attacked as unfair, thus inappropriate.

Curiously, fairness has in an explicit form come late to the common law. In terms of fair dealing it has now invaded the sanctity of the law of contract, first in the United States and then elsewhere in the common law world. It is now embodied in the Vienna Convention on the Sale of Goods. See M. V. Ellis, "The Fuss About Fairness: Good Faith and Fair Dealing in the International Arena," *National Bank and Law Review,* X, ii, 1991.

son. If there were some objective, fair, or just price, economic exchange itself would make no sense.

(Forbes, March 16, 1992).

With respect to the formulation of foreign policy, judgment demands that a state not be blinded by ideology but attend to its specific effects. In a paper (1964) delivered in India in the hey-day of Third World neutralism I submitted that judgments on the adoption of such a policy must be state-to-state specific and informed by the geopolitical priorities of the country concerned. Both papers (1964 and 1968) argue that policy judgments go astray by adherence to concepts without zeroing in on conse-quences which may conflict with the paramount interests of the parties at stake.

In systems where party discipline is strict, rather than policy formation the chief task of backbenchers is primarily to sell the party's position and ensure its election.[73] And in the age of tele-vision image has become critical to electoral success. But image is not a given; it is created from the substance of opinions and also from dozens of seemingly trivial subsidiary judgments of facial expression, walk, tone of voice, and dress. Such judgments start out as those of a politician and end up as our judgment of the politician's. Judgments of image gradually evolve into judgment of personality and therefore credibility. Credibility in politics depends on the same factors as in the everyday, writ large. So impressions of leadership depend on image created from judg-ment displayed in countless newsbites.

Aristotle felt that politics was the fullest realization of pru-dence, that is practical wisdom. He thought of Pericles as prudent because he could envisage what was good for people in general, much as he could envisage what was good for himself. Ultimately politics is a practical exercise that hangs on the taking

---

73. We are now far removed from Burke's ideal of the elected repre-sentative not being swayed by the dictates of either party or polls: "Your representative owes you, not his industry only, but his judgment; and he betrays instead of serving you if he sacrifices it to your opinion" *(To the Electors of Bristol,* 1774).

of a particular deliberative step. Yet with respect to the formulation of policy, values and creativity are the starting point.

Doubtless, ideas are the life of statecraft but they are also its death: the convenient cover they provide hides irregularities, which invites abuse. Take the "idea" of planning and its negative analogue deregulation. Think of the havoc caused by their indiscriminate application to countryside, neighborhoods, and savings institutions. It is the very power of ideas which warns of taking them too solemnly—the power of being easily grasped, married, and passed on.[74] So ideas thrown up must pass through the filter of judgment on extent and fit, where other ideas on means again enter in.[75] Seeing judgments as *decisions* rather than as ongoing states of mind (and thus dependent upon different causal families) prepares us for the instability that attends politics for good or ill. Hence the surprise brought by the flash of change that lights up the world when immutable policies are overthrown.

Examples of bad political judgment abound. In Canada one thinks of the well-intentioned Kennedyesque social programs of the

---

74. Michael Oakeshott (1967) is getting at much the same thing in his account of the practice of politics but he rests it on the well-worn distinction between technical knowledge (book learning, laws, principles) and practical knowledge (analogous to practical reason discussed earlier). To label the exercise of judgment (a concept he curiously neglects) as a parallel kind of *knowledge* is misleading on several counts. All knowledge carries with it an aura of generalization, even the knowledge of particulars. It raises expectations of predictability and implication. This is so even in instances of "knowing how." If someone knows how to play hockey, we can confidently say that the player knows how to skate and perhaps bodycheck. But how a player executes a particular play is not knowledge, nothing flows from it. So it is with the plays of exercising judgment. Of course, to borrow Hilary Putnam's phrase to different effect, judgment is "in the head," whereas "knowing how" to play hockey is in the bones and thus perhaps not any kind of knowledge at all.

75. The opposite view is attributed to utopians by Isaiah Berlin: "Where ends are agreed, the only questions left are those of means, and these are not political but technical, that is to say, capable of being settled by experts or machines like arguments between engineers or doctors" (1969, 118). About engineers and doctors, though, see comments above under "Other Professions," which suggest no such clear demarcation.

early 1970s: the Council of Young Canadians, the Local Initiative Program, amendments to the Unemployment Insurance Act. It is now conceded that what went wrong was not the far-reaching ideas themselves; it was a failure of perspective, of allocation of weights, of the tests of appropriateness, ultimately a disregard of the particulars.

In the United States one thinks of a string of bad judgments in foreign policy in the post-war years (North Korea, Bay of Pigs, Vietnam). Irving Janis has attributed these to "groupthink":

> The poor decision-making performance of the men at those White House meetings might be akin to the lapses in judgment of ordinary citizens who become more concerned with retaining the approval of the fellow members of their work group than with coming up with good solutions to the tasks at hand. . . . These observations began to fit a specific pattern of concurrence-seeking behavior that had impressed me time and again in my research on other kinds of face-to-face groups, particularly when a "we-feeling" of solidarity is running high.
>
> (1972, iii)

The environment will remain a frontline concern. No area is more riddled with judgmental issues than this. Here perspective is everything. Should the survival of one species of fish (the snail darter) stop the completion of a costly dam? Should the survival of the spotted owl block the logging of old forests?[76] Or take the common circumstance where n dollars will remove 95 percent of the contamination in a location and $10n$ dollars is required to remove the remaining 5 percent.[77] What to do? The answer can be

---

76. See the discussion by Ronald Dworkin (1986, 13) of the Snail Darter decision of the U.S. Supreme Court.

77. An analogy from health care is given by research that indicates that heart attack victims given TPA rather than streptokinase have a 1 percent greater chance of a month's survival. But TPA costs ten times more than streptokinase. This is not simply life versus cash. Rather, the teaser is to come to grips with the appropriate measure to assess "life" and "money" taken by themselves. A TPA backer said: "It is highly significant to have ten patients in a thousand survive, or two thousand in the U.S. a year" (*Wall Street Journal*, May 3, 1993). Is the right frame your family, your community, or your country?

given only by a judgment on the interplay of considerations on the particular facts. But because such an *ad hoc* process is not amenable to generalization or slogans, compromise and discretion need to be worked into the body of environmental regulations at a cost to predictability. To some extent this already appears in the language of some legislation. Thus enforcement for breach of pollution regulations will depend on *significant* or *substantial* noncompliance.[78]

This century has reinforced the conviction that no evil is greater than institutionalized evil. It is harder to accept that good cannot be institutionalized. The seeming departures from this negative conclusion are techniques for dismantling institutions that have gone wrong. Beyond this, attempts to legislate positive morality endanger the paramount ideal of fairness, to judge each case on its merits, albeit with heightened objectivity. And the degree to which such institutional interventions are justified with respect to a class of concerns is in itself a central judgmental issue.

That is not to say that positive morality has no place in politics. I discuss the dilemma of moral directions in politics later but there is also the morality of a commitment to the process. We saw that in the professions the threshold level of expert knowledge required is sometimes sufficiently low not to deter us from exercising our own judgment. With respect to politics this must be taken further. Politics is thought of as the affair of others, as a profession, an avocation, and a right to be exercised on election day. But what about our ongoing participation, indeed our moral commitment to the process? Morality is usually seen *negatively.* Don't lie, don't steal, don't break your promises. The *positive* obligations of morality are difficult to define. Witness the trite quandary of determining the appropriate amounts and objects of

---

78. I am not here suggesting that the presence of concepts such as significant, substantial, material, and reasonable scattered throughout the law gives the courts a discretion. A court has the duty to determine as a fact whether the matter at hand is significant, substantial and so on. What is to be noted is that the determination of this class of facts exhibits on its face the judgmental elements involved, which lie concealed under the determination of facts in general.

annual charitable donations. At the other extreme, whether to intervene militarily in distant countries throws considerations of weight and appropriateness into high relief. There is the golden rule, but how far do our obligations under it extend? In this shrunken world who is *not* my neighbor?

Ernst Tugendhat has put forward the view (1987 John Dewey Lecture, Columbia University) that participation in politics is the expression of our moral duty. He sees politics as the necessary extension of the moral dimension. It is through our political commitment that we discharge our positive moral obligations. It is thus only in a small but real way that we can give effect to what underlies the Rule. We are obliged to engage ourselves[79] in pursuit of our ideals at the appropriate level, in the appropriate way.[80] What perhaps also follows is that the content of politics becomes more diffuse. If we stretch our ideals beyond rights and material distribution, rights may not always get their due. We may end up taking them less strictly because of our commitment to some ideal that does not lend itself to such encapsulation and we can

---

79. The deadening consequences of nonparticipation are seen by Charles Taylor (1991, 9): "But there is another kind of loss of freedom, which has also been widely discussed, most memorably by Alexis de Tocqueville. A society in which people end up as the kind of individuals who are 'enclosed in their own hearts' is one where few will want to participate actively in self-government. They will prefer to stay at home and enjoy the satisfactions of private life, as long as the government of the day produces the means to these satisfactions and distributes them widely. This opens the danger of a new, specifically modern form of despotism which Tocqueville calls 'soft' despotism."

80. Determining *the appropriate level* requires a distinction between what is properly the subject of *public* rights and what should remain private. As Jean Elshtain (1993, 41) points out, "All is defined as 'political' and watered down to the lowest common denominator . . . everything I 'want' gets defined politically as a 'right.' This notion means my desire, now a right, to have easy access to a pornography channel on cable television is conflated to my right to be safe from arbitrary search and seizure. Authentic civil rights get trivialized in this process. Political ideals and private desires are blurred or collapsed. By extension, of course, there is no such thing as an authentically private sphere. Intimate life is pervaded with politics; private identity becomes a recommendation for, or authentication of, one's political stance."

outwit the tyranny of abstractions (George Woodcock's phrase), not by shunning them but by putting them into the service of applications we deem right. Such an approach changes the debate between liberals and conservatives and in a wider sense between both and communitarians.

Art

We say that politics is an art, or the art of the possible. We often say that the practice of a particular profession, say economic forecasting, or rendering an appropriate account for legal services, is more art than science. Of course we don't mean that it is an art. What we are alluding to is the cardinal place of judgment in these pursuits. But if politics is thought of as an art,[81] what of art itself? How does judgment apply?

In the creation of art, judgment in the sense described enters late. Without here considering what constitutes the creative process or the recalcitrant cases of genius, it is clear from the general practice of artists in working over the original material, that they are exercising a critical process. This is not a judgmen-

---

81. Hannah Arendt, on the other hand, seems to say that art is a kind of politics when she seeks "to classify taste, the chief cultural activity, among man's political abilities" (Arendt 1977, 222–23):

Taste judgments . . . share with political opinions that they are persuasive; the judging person—as Kant says quite beautifully—can only "woo the consent of everyone else" in the hope of coming to an agreement with him eventually. . . . Culture and politics, then, belong together because it is not knowledge or truth which is at stake, but rather judgment and decision, the judicious exchange of opinion about the sphere of public life and the common world, and the decision what manner of action is to be taken in it, as well as how it is to look henceforth, what kind of things are to appear in it.

One thinks as well of Jakob Burckhardt's image of the renaissance city-state as a work of art.

tal process easily available to others.[82] It entails a determination of the importance and appropriateness of every feature unique not only to the medium but to the artist's intention. Aristotle tells us, "It is customary to say of well-executed works that nothing can be added to them or taken away, the implication being that excess and deficiency alike destroy perfection" (*Ethics* II.vi.1106b). Perhaps, but this observation comes too easily after the event. While theories abound on what goes into the making, judgment of the creation is inescapable.

Thus the concept of art brings with it the concept of criticism.[83] Art is simply the most obvious domain where criticism is itself conceptualized. Criticism is an example of evaluative judgment that examines and passes on a subject sometimes against a set of standards, values, or rules. In a larger sense it is the application of these criteria to a specific event that constitutes the control mechanism we have over our beliefs in a given area. In the discussion of evaluative judgments later on, the central place of background knowledge will become evident.

Yet applying the tests of importance and appropriateness to art gives odd results. *Appropriateness* is inextricably related to matters of form and relationships, which in a sense is what art is about. The work is as form a statement of the appropriateness of the internal elements. It may also be a statement of an intentionality relationship to external elements such as social and other ideas. In either

---

82. Arendt further discusses Kant's conception of the respective places of genius and judgment in art (1978, 261):

In the discussion of aesthetic judgment, the distinction is between genius which is required for the production of art works, while for judging them, and deciding whether or not they are beautiful objects, "no more" (we would say, but not Kant) is required than taste. "For judging of beautiful objects *taste* is required. . . . For their production *genius* is required." Genius according to Kant is a matter of productive imagination and originality, taste a matter of judgment.

83. And editing. Edward Mendelson, Auden's literary executor, quotes him: "I let my friends do my punctuation for me." Mendelson adds, "You lose sleep over it, but you have to decide one way or another. Let me rephrase that. You have to use your judgment." (*Wall Street Journal,* January 20, 1994)

case the reference to appropriateness is anomalous in the sense of seeming to attend to a secondary quality. It is the main event.[84]

There is, however, much talk of *importance* with respect to art. The best thing you can say about a work is that it is important. We venture beyond straightforward attributes of value (excellent, beautiful) to allude to something structural. Underlying all judgments on the comparative greatness of art are appeals to intuitions of importance. Within the work itself, we think of the importance assigned to individual elements, or the suppression of importance as in say, the painting of Vuillard. But beyond the artist's ordering within the work is the fiat to the priority of the work itself. What is most moving in music is perhaps the conviction of importance with which the composer invests a series of odd notes. Wallace Stevens observed in *The Necessary Angel*:

> We do not have to be told the significance of art. "It is art," said Henry James, "which makes life, makes interest, *makes importance* . . . and I know of no substitute whatever for the force and beauty of its process."
>
> (quoted by Sukenick, 1967, 35; emphasis mine)

There is discovery but there is also satisfaction in recognition, a sharing of priorities. Part of a reader's pleasure is an acknowledgment that what is written is *worth* being written about,[85] worth in the sense of being important. Conversely, when we lay aside a

---

84. "The artist's answers are appeals to our sense of fitness or harmony" (Roger Fry 1939, 30).

85. Or worth being loved. Benjamin Constant's *Adolphe*: "Mon coeur avait besoin d'amour . . . un conquête digne de moi" (My heart needed love . . . a conquest worthy of myself). And its complement: "But the deepest forms of erotic love involve a longing for the lover's recognition of something more than one's physical characteristics, a longing for what amounts to a recognition of one's worth" (Fukuyama 1992, 176).

Fukuyama recalls Nietzsche's melancholy observation: "No artist will paint his picture, no general win his victory, no nation gain its freedom . . . without loving the work that they do infinitely more than it deserves to be loved" (1992, 306).

Emerson says: "The worth of the thing signified must vindicate our taste for the emblem" (1883, 148). Here quality and importance merge.

half-read book it is because it does not touch, even in a tangential way, anything worth the craft. Such worth may lie in the after-ring of a universal theme sounded by treatment of exemplars,[86] or in the insights of a Lady Murasaki, Proust, or Forster. This semiconscious recognition that what is written is worthwhile, important, comes through the treatment given the particular. So judgment dedicated to the treatment of the particular case is integral to the artistic process. Art is a paean to the particular.

It would seem to follow that criticism should retain its focus on the particular, the work. Not so for critical theory and its antecedents which fix on circumstances surrounding its birth under cover of textual analysis. But isn't this methodology a misreading of what the nature of the material requires to be taken into account as important and appropriate? All art is to be taken at face value. What the face displays can itself be particularized by acute comment. Appeal to a depersonalized artistic intent may be in order. Beyond some point judgment and discipline need curb the stray into remote territory. Remote considerations are just those inappropriate to see the autonomy of the work radiating its own values.[87]

---

86. But portrayed in and for themselves. Theodor Adorno is said to have remarked that in the last century Germans attempted to paint their dreams and only succeeded in painting vegetables, while the French set out to paint vegetables and created dreams.

87. Remoteness also figures in the law of contract and tort. The legal principle of remoteness of damage provides, for example, if damages for negligence are remote, they are not recoverable. There have been two theories that have fought for supremacy on how remoteness is to be established. One is to trace the causal chain until the link is broken. The other is to determine whether the damages in question were reasonably foreseeable by the defendant. Either way the principle provides a salutary exclusion of *inappropriate* classes of damage from recovery and hence a containment to litigation.

The Commercial Edifice

The professional investor and economist scan the broad tape or computer screen for the latest announcement of the producer price index and trade deficit figures for the previous month. The *Wall Street Journal* then quotes their "interpretation" of the figures to mean that the dollar will rise against the basket of European currencies. The language of interpretation to describe what the professional investor or economist is doing masks the function that is being performed. To be sure, *interpretation* is required to determine the expanded meaning of the statistics by examining the components of the producer price index and concluding that 20 percent of the increase was due to an increase in the price of copper. So much is simply a matter of understanding the complex of words and numbers. But to go on to realize that the increase in the price of copper was due to a strike in Chile and that its resolution will lead to a reduction in the copper price component in next month's index, which in turn may indicate a lessening of inflation, involves a thought process beyond interpretation.

Assuming the investor or economist makes a judgment that the causal effect of a reduction in the copper price will be to reduce interest rates, she then must make a further judgment as to whether currency traders will be bullish on the dollar because of the reduction in inflationary pressures and therefore the stability of the currency, or bearish on the dollar because interest rates will go down and the yields on short-term dollar denominated investments will be reduced, thereby making such investments less attractive.

What the investor and economist are doing is not *interpreting* the significance of the statistics. This is not a heuristic exercise of determining the meaning of a text. They are conducting a multi-level causal analysis that is misleading to label as interpretation. For example, judgments of future price movements are made more complex because the crosscurrents generated by the perceptions of the judgments of others must themselves be correlated. The troublemaker is "significance" which can mean either the meaning of an expression, including its emotional coloration (the subject of interpretation), or, what *other* belief (or conclusion) the expression would lead us to hold (the subject of judgment).

Economic indicators are notorious for pointing to conflicting conclusions. The quandary of predicting the consequences of reduction in the producer price index is an example of the inherent ambiguity of economic indicators. They point at least two ways because for every action there is a perceived reaction, for every trend a countertrend. The direction pointed by an event is a function of the judgment on selecting the appropriate time frame. A central bank raises the interest rate. From a short-term view, because it signals inflationary pressure, it may drive the stock market down. From a long-term view, it may indicate that the central bank is standing up to inflation and may drive the market up. The reactions include those of investors and governments. The *Wall Street Journal* reminds us every day of the Janus-faced nature of data. A headline reads, "Good News on U.S. Economy Sends Markets Down." The explanation was that the news suggested higher interest rates. Or conversely,

> Stocks moved higher following a report that the nation's unemployment surged to 6.5% in February, the highest rate since 1987. The evidence of marked economic weakness raised hopes that the Federal Reserve would lower interest rates.

For every bit of good or bad news there is the offsetting consideration to what extent it has been discounted in the market. There are always conflicting considerations on what the present price of a stock holds for the future. The most conspicuous manifestation is the judgment of the *appropriate* ratio of the price of a stock to the estimate of its future earnings.

Crosscurrents of judgments create eddies that even disappointed expectations will not explain. According to the *Wall Street Journal*:

> Delta Air posted a bigger-than-expected quarterly loss due to discount wars and high costs on new European routes. The results could foreshadow a bleak year for the industry. But Delta stock rose $2.625 to $60.50.

Or a headline in the Toronto *Globe and Mail* reads: "U.S. Dollar Closes Down Amid Rumors of Federal Reserve Buying." The putative reasoning is that the market thought that the fundamental forces affecting the dollar must be bearish if the Federal Reserve Board believed it necessary to intervene. Or consider the fact that the day after the 1989 San Francisco earthquake, insurance stocks shot up rather than plummeting in the face of a 10-billion-dollar estimate of damage. Again the explanation was that somehow the extensive damage would lead to lifting depressed insurance premium rates. These seeming anomalies can be explained in theory by positing a more sophisticated causal analysis leading to one result rather than another. But such causal analyses depend upon probability judgments that are far from mathematical. Indeed, the stock market provides a paradigm case of the effect of differing judgments on the same information.[88]

Years ago it may have made sense to say that the investor or economist who had the best information made the best predictions. But the continuing emphasis on information taken by itself is now misconceived.[89] In the age of databanks and computer screens that provide instantaneous transmission of information, mere knowledge is a constant, common to all professional decisions. It is because insider information is the exception that proves the rule, that it has produced such a hullabaloo. But even insider information is not always the exception. In 1989, executives at four New England banks sustained large paper losses as stocks they bought in their own banks plunged. Presumably these insiders had the best information. The fault lay in their judgment.

---

88. A vivid example was the initial judgment of the market on news of a slight reduction of the German discount rate, which is said to have sent the Dow Jones Industrial Average up 70 points. The next day the market is said to have had second thoughts and dropped 49 points. As the *Globe and Mail* columnist said, "The world has not changed."

89. Quarterly earnings first come to mind. In order to make assessments and comparisons, normalized earnings are sought. But where financial reports are peppered with "extraordinary" or "nonrecurring" items, how are we to weigh them and what credibility is left to earnings as a benchmark of a company's value?

Some studies have shown that advisory services that track insider trades and recommended purchases and sales of stocks accordingly have fared poorer than average.

So the variable that accounts for predictive success is not information but the weight placed on one bit of information as against another, which in turn depends on perceptions of importance. The process appears to be either highly complex or possibly extremely simple. Market feel may be an unconscious shorthand for such process. Or it may be a stray insight that one fact is all important. For every professional judgment that a particular stock or currency should be sold another professional makes the opposite judgment and buys. It is because information is so widely disseminated that differing judgments as to its effect must be taken to account for contrary decisions. That the market price is simply the outcome of demand and supply does not itself illuminate such contrary decisions. Demand and supply with respect to most goods is determined by both physical need and considerations of future price movements. What distinguishes the special case of securities and other instances of speculation is that the physical need for the goods is absent (except for covering by short sellers). So what remains to determine demand and supply is a pure conflict of considerations balanced on the knife edge of market price.

The phenomenon of arbitrage lives on divergent judgments. For example, closed-end funds that invest in the securities of a particular country with similar portfolios may at times trade at premiums in some markets and discounts in others. The fact that arbitrage works to reduce these discrepancies does not mean that the same judgment comes to govern. It is rather that different judgments are made on the intrinsic value and a second-order judgment preys on the resulting discrepancy.

It is this double-edged phenomenon, the ubiquity of economic information yet its insufficiency taken by itself, that makes the "efficient market" hypothesis and the modern portfolio or "random walk" theory silly. Theorists who embrace these positions contend that as stock market prices instantaneously reflect all available information, success in beating the market averages can only be attributed to luck. The theory is based on the assumption that bits of information in themselves are the critical ingredient in market decisions; given the same information, investors will make the same judgments. We know that markets often change dramatically in minutes without new informational input. It also assumes manifest causal connections. Hume would smile at the easy attribution of cause and effect to account for market moves cited in the daily press. We also know that a significant number of investors beat the market consistently for significant periods of time to a degree inconsistent with luck. That most of them do not maintain their winning streak over long periods or in different phases of the market simply indicates that the peculiar process of forming their judgments which work in some phases may not work in others, that judgment is fallible.

The evidence of these individual successes and failures also brings into question whether there is any one theory on how to win on Wall Street. Many have been put forward: the averaging-down theory, the low price/earnings ratio theory, the growth stock theory, contrarian theories, the target-point sale theory as against the let-profits-run theory, and so forth. Then there are the technical theories that disregard "fundamentals" and look solely at the price and volume trends of the market or of a particular stock. The pure technician professes to predict the price of the market or stock from the pattern established by past prices and volumes. But none are known to have submitted to the simple test of predicting the next moves that were in fact made by an arbitrarily selected stock plotted on a partially covered chart of past prices and trading volumes. It is not surprising that none of these systems have been proved right or even reliably good guides to investing. That is so because investment choice depends on judgment which by definition must be tailor-made to conform to the particular conditions at hand to accomplish a particular objective. No general theory will be right most of the time. The trick is to know which theory, guideline or consideration is appropriate at a particular time and at what point to tap into the vast causal matrix. We have seen that information itself is the beginning and not the end of the investment decision. The investor will take the information and borrow one of the theories that may carry him through a particular phase of the market. The fact that there are few agile enough to change course successfully over a long period does not invalidate the conclusion that judgment with respect to individual decisions is critical to investment success.

John Train describes one of the most agile, and captures the judgmental nature of money management in his discussion of Peter Lynch:

> How can it be that a single individual, virtually without a staff, and managing an enormous mass of capital—the $10-billion Magellan Fund—greatly outperforms a large, able organization, the best that the governing body of an old and famous institution can assemble, handling only a fraction as much money? That is, how does Peter Lynch do so much better than his neighbors at Harvard Management? The chief reason is that a supremely capable individual—and Peter Lynch is one—easily outmaneuvers a large committee which essentially describes Harvard Management. Wellington, who never lost a battle, also never held councils of war. . . .
>
> The essence of Lynch's technique is *fluency,* letting his portfolio flow easily from one idea to another. He notices some apparent opportunity in the market and moves on it forthwith, without delaying for extensive analysis. Of course, this requires both flair and a sure judgment based on a long experience of the subject. One is reminded of superb generalship; at Salamanca, Wellington watches Marmont marching parallel to him across a valley. Suddenly he spots an advantage. "By God! That'll do."[90]

Or take the description of another fund manager:

> His approach is intuitive, impossible to categorize. The widely assorted ideas in his portfolio reflect virtually all known investment disciplines: growth, value, turnarounds, and, on the

---

90. John Train, *The New Money Masters* (New York: Harper & Row, 1989), p. 192.

short side, excessive leverage. Robertson is open to all ideas—
but he runs them through the computer that is his mind before
he accepts or rejects them.[91]

Hence a word on *intuition,* often associated by writers with
judgment. Like market feel, intuition refers either to the intellectual dead end beyond which analysis cannot be pushed, or to a
decision in which the judgmental process has been telescoped.
Rather than reducing judgment to intuition, what is useful is to
locate the intuitional elements in both these senses in the judgmental process.

Success seems tied to the particular. What appears to account
for the long-term success of investors such as Warren Buffett and
Benjamin Graham may be a mere handful of decisions. Graham
is said to have reflected, "One supremely shrewd decision may
account for more than a lifetime of journeyman efforts." Yet a
1992 academic study has supported what we would expect, past
performance is a reasonable basis for predicting future performance (Mark Hulbert, *Forbes,* May 25 and August 17, 1992).
Both Buffett and Graham realized that the essence of detecting
"values" in stock selection lies in the weighting process in particular instances.

When we move from the stock market itself to consider the
performance of financial institutions, it is the counterexample of
bad judgment that is startling. It was a failure of applying the criteria of importance and appropriateness that led to money-center
banks in the 1970s and 1980s making excessive loans to Third
World countries and to finance domestic leveraged buy-outs such
as the Campeau takeover of the Federated and Allied department
store chains. The same approach can be laid at the door of
investment bankers, one of the softest professions, who advise
clients with respect to mergers and acquisitions. The failures of
the transactions structured by them were not due to technical factors such as faulty security. It was judgment on the large issues

---

91. Article on Julian Robertson by Frederick E. Rowe, Jr., "The Best
Instincts in the Jungle," *Forbes,* September 16, 1991.

which determine risk that went wrong. In the collapse of the Olympia & York empire it was betting the ranch on continued inflation and tenant demand for office space in the London docklands.[92] On these issues the record does not give ground for confidence that the judgment of those within the financial community was better than those without.

Nor are the regulators of the financial system immune. It was one act of judgment, of characterization, that was the culprit for the severity of the 1987 stock market crash. Stock index futures, a second order derivative investment instrument, escaped the margin and other rules imposed by the Securities and Exchange Commission because such instruments were characterized as *commodities* rather than *securities*. Thus unlimited leverage and uncontrolled selling were permitted which led to the severity of the decline. Such derivatives along with puts, calls, options, and swaps (and derivatives of derivatives) which have dominated the financial markets, while useful to hedge risk by off-balance sheet transactions, require judgments beyond accounting, to determine whether one is seeing in financial statements financial reality or virtual reality.

Throughout I have assumed the concept of success as a criterion of good judgment in investment or commercial decisions. One would naturally assume that *success* is the conceptual safe-haven in deciding all academic questions relating to commerce, the touchstone that quells all doubts. On reflection its very meaning is by no means self-evident. Its meaning is dependent on the question that is being asked. Did the price of the security or portfolio go up or down in the past six months, six years, or twenty years?[93] Is the gain before or after taxes? Is the future payment of

---

92. In a domino effect the misjudgments of the world's largest real estate developer brings in its train large political judgments: "Can a Tory government [U.K.] committed to free enterprise afford—politically or economically—to bail out a big developer? Can it afford not to?" (*Wall Street Journal,* May 18, 1992)

93. This judgmental issue intrudes into the law. Where there has been an unauthorized investment of a security at an alleged loss, how do you determine its quantum—by noting its price the next day, month, or year?

taxes on accrued gains to be discounted? In what currency is the
gain or loss to be measured? Take the case of an investor from
Britain, Australia, or Canada who invests half his funds in securities of his own country and half on Wall Street. Both do equally well domestically. After five years the investor's domestic currency has fallen in value against the United States dollar. How
does he measure his success? In terms of his domestic currency
he has been eminently successful in his home country and to the
degree that the proceeds of his total portfolio will be used to
finance an enterprise there, the fall of his currency in relation to
the dollar will increase the proceeds of his U.S. investments. He
will congratulate himself on his astuteness in investing half his
portfolio on Wall Street and bemoan the failure to invest the other
half likewise. Or should an American who has done well on the
Street discount his winnings because he may retire in Japan?

It is also said that a different sort of qualification should be
added to success as a measure of investment judgment: risk taking. How much risk was assumed in achieving a certain level of
performance? What is meant by risk? Is it risk relating to the
business or to the level of valuation of the stock regardless of the
business?[94] In either case discounting for risk drains the life out
of the concept of investment success. So we see the yardstick of
success disintegrate. The only guides available are the concepts
of importance and appropriateness to ask the proper questions.
Yet, intuition tells us that in the face of massive individual success these academic quibbles would meet the same fate as solip-
sism did at Doctor Johnson's foot.[95]

Society has thus produced two fascinating paradigms of judgment: the stock market and litigation. In both, the results are
inherently uncertain. Yet it makes sense to put forward arguments
in advance why a certain result should obtain. Both may result in
different judgments on the same facts. Both involve a contest

---

94. Stock market theorists equate risk with volatility indicated by the
beta factor. But isn't risk simply the measure of the probability of loss
which is to be determined together with all other factors by an independent
act of judgment?

95. See the reference to Richard Wilbur's poem under "Cognition."

between adversarial parties. Both systems have been refined to provide all sides access to the same information going into the contest. In litigation it is through pretrial sworn discoveries and the delivery of documentation. In the stock market it is the rules that govern insider trading, the dissemination of material information, and stop-trading orders. In both the measure of success must have a time horizon. In litigation, although the results for a particular party are ultimately determined when the appeal process runs out, the establishment of the legal principle may never be conclusively settled. In the stock market, success is always relative to some alternate result over some arbitrarily determined period. In both, commentators dispense much wisdom after the event.

If still within the commercial edifice we move over one academic notch to examine predictions of professional economists with respect to macroeconomic trends, the record is not encouraging. Stephen McNees, vice-president of the Federal Reserve Bank of Boston, matched the prediction of a representative group of economic forecasters against what happened. He found in the period between 1970 and 1990 that predictions of Gross National Product growth and inflation at times when economic direction changed were wildly inaccurate. Moreover, the predictions of these economists appeared to cluster together. The reason may be that the predictions were simply extrapolations of past trends that served fairly well where there is little change in the underlying economic factors. But where such changes did occur, that is in those circumstances where professional judgment would be expected to provide answers (where the answers could not be read off an econometric model), it provided none. Hence the trend to shed economists by business. It is not surprising that the predictions of economists with respect to microeconomic events are more accurate. The more micro, the more particular, the clearer the causal links.

The poor performance of economic models is in part due to the dilemma of choosing the right measuring sticks. The shifting definition of money that guides the governors of central banks and the varied emphasis that is given to M1, M2, M3 as measures of money supply is an example. Which is the appropriate test? And when is it relevant to take as a guide gross national product in nominal terms or in "real" inflation-adjusted terms? The results in gauging the severity of a recession are quite different. So it is with measuring inflation. Which commodity, producer, and consumer price indexes, all with different ingredients and weights, does one choose? An institutional money manager is faced with an array of conflicting statistics. The average real annual rate of return for Canadian common stocks for the fifty-year period 1941 to 1990 was 6.59 percent. For the ten-year period 1981 to 1990 the return was 1.85 percent. But by moving the ten-year period by just one year to 1982 to 1991 it was 4.95 percent. Which period's performance (fifty, twenty-five, or the last ten years) is more relevant in predicting the return during the *next* ten years?[96]

In a larger sense, the last hurdle in economic prediction is causal weighting. Ever more subtle analysis has isolated the causal crosscurrents leading to persuasive explanations of recalcitrant phenomena. Why, say, a weakening currency should go along with a widening trade deficit. After the event we may be led to a convincing story of what happened but we can only conclude vacuously that one set of causes must have overwhelmed another. Before the event, what success in predictability is possible will thus depend finally on judgments on causal weighting.

While straight-line economic rationality is no longer attributed by economists to individuals, nonetheless that assumption lingers and affects expectations about economic prediction. Think of the asymmetry of attitudes to losing (spending) $10 and gaining $10. Here we learn more from Balzac than from decision theory. The psychology of money is yet to be written. What it will reveal is the gap between the complex explanations of discrete conduct and statistical generalities. It will also reveal that the commercial edifice would crumble if the chinks in certainty with which it is riddled were not mortared by trust. We think nothing of signing a receipt at a teller's window before we are handed the cash. From there the uncertainties compound to be weighted and rated.

---

96. Canadian Institute of Actuaries, *Report on Canadian Economic Statistics,* 1991.

We know that action can be taken by central banks to weaken or strengthen the domestic currency or increase or reduce interest rates and that governments can generally take actions to stimulate or dampen the economy. But again what is the measure of success? In a more general sense that runs through all matters of social import and goes to the root of pragmatism, how do we tell if something works? The time frame will determine the picture. If one can effect direction but has no objective measurement of result it becomes hazardous to make the attempt. The targets in any economic strategy are ultimately hostage to a concept of success. To the extent that such a concept is definable ultimately by appeals to criteria of appropriateness and importance, that yardstick softens accordingly. The fallout for policymakers is caution in pushing economic levers that may lead in a known direction but with no clear way of knowing whether the target has been under or overshot.

Finally, judgment enters the commercial edifice on issues of corporate responsibility to the community on environmental, worker welfare, and other ethically tinged matters. It is often said that responsibility of this sort can apply only to natural persons. It is said that corporations ultimately act through natural persons and therefore it is a misuse of language to ascribe such concepts to fictional or artificial entities, a sort of pathetic fallacy. It is argued that the market, driven ultimately by the economic and moral demands of individual consumers, will resolve all ethical issues.

It should be observed that the ingenious Anglo-American invention of the corporation in the mid-nineteenth century has resulted in a pronounced built-in bias toward success for investors in the stock market. Until corporations became the norm an investor in a business not only risked losing his investment but going bankrupt. A creditor could pursue the personal assets of not only active but silent partners. While disgrace replaced debtors' prison, both the upside and the downside remained unlimited. The corporation provided the ironclad floor to risk, leaving the ceiling of possible profit unlimited.

Now, what is responsible for this insulation of the investor from the losses of the corporation since the 1897 English House of Lords decision in *Salomon* v *Salomon* is the legal fiat that the corporation is a distinct person, that *it* has incurred the obligation, not the shareholder. Furthermore, many of the statutes, charters, or articles of Western legal systems that create these legal creatures explicitly attribute to corporations some or all the powers of a natural person. And we commonly talk of actions being taken by corporations themselves rather than by the president or the board of directors. In most cases it would not make sense to ascribe such conduct in any other way. That being so, why then if a corporation exercises certain of the powers of a natural person should it not also have the responsibilities and obligations of a natural person that go with such exercise?[97] Of course, just as there are certain powers that cannot be performed other than by natural persons, so it is with responsibilities and obligations. But many can. So judgments as to the responsibility of corporations to the community cannot be dismissed out of hand on logical grounds. While a host of other considerations may well apply to determine the content of such obligations, ultimately the judgmental process to determine corporate responsibility does not differ from moral judgments generally.

But moral judgments are not to be confused with the generic judgments which need follow. The director of a target company subject to a takeover bid may be firm in his determination to do the right thing for the company and its shareholders. Once that legal and moral decision has been made, the hard judgment required is whether accepting the bid or launching a costly defensive move best meets the legal and moral test.

So the building blocks of the commercial edifice (including of course the underlying businesses themselves) consist of a flux

---

97. Corporations are just one sort of organization to which these considerations apply. Organizations are defined by Argyris and Schön (1978) as a government or *polis,* an agency and a task system which can itself make decisions. The authors have in that book and in their earlier *Theory in Practice* (1974) discussed how to improve effectiveness of action and decisions for managers and professionals without, however, discussing the role of judgment and its ingredients of weighting and fitting.

of judgments of risk, weight, and structural regularity itself. Which features do we pick to determine regularity? Taking advantage of anomalies in the market seems a fruitful investment strategy. But anomalies assume regularity. Even the image of business cycles is simplistic. The ups and downs of different segments of the economy follow different paths. Yet some predictions work. Hence, an instance of the pervasive dilemma facing social theory: How far to take our crystallizations of the past in the form of rules, formulas, and models?

Social Policy

The preceding comments on the indeterminacy of the effects of political and economic decisions prompt consideration of social policy in general. At the outset we should note that there is something to both sides of most interesting sociopolitical arguments. That's what makes them interesting. Take the decision of Britain to enter Europe or the referenda on the conditions of European monetary and political union or the proposed constitutional amendment limiting terms of members of the United States Congress. Or consider the two issues that have riven Canada: the constitutional issue relating to the status of Quebec, and the Free Trade Agreement with the United States and later Mexico. In neither case was one side able to deliver an intellectual knockout punch to the other. Now in both these issues it is possible to postulate a hypothetical observer of good will who appreciates the values underlying *both* sides of the argument. How then should such an observer reach a decision? It must lie in the weight that is attributed to the respective elements and, to the extent events are involved, differing probability determinations. In a larger sense, these political examples can be seen as a subclass of a wider judgmental process where "values" are simply the brand names given to the considerations that move us within the argument one way or another.

In the above scenario the observer accepts *all* the values. Where the sharing is minimal, it is the grain of truth in the other's position that irritates—or the other's blindness to see it so. But what comes through in these cases is not simply the indispensability of the weighting function but the diminished role assigned to the *conflict* of values. Perhaps this growing disinterest in such conflict is attributable to our primary values being biologically wired into us, as Pugh (1977) thought, and to a sufficiently common experiential base to produce sufficiently common secondary and tertiary values that underlie policy issues. In any event, ending up with the same basket of values becomes an empty victory where everything hangs on the ordering, the weight given to each in the specific situation that calls for a particular decision.

In spite of the evidence of the convergence of social values, sufficient differences remain to pose profound dilemmas of weighting, both economic and moral. One such, endemic to the issue, is the judgment of other societies—aboriginal pockets in our society and more generally the specter of the North/South impasse. How to steer between a sloppy relativism and a prissy self-righteousness? What allowances should we make? World standards or local standards? How far to stretch our objectivity to tolerate political and social values repugnant to or merely inconsistent with our own? While the judgmental issue is only too obvious in the moral sphere, it crops up unobtrusively in the *appreciation* of social products where empathy and insight may still call for judgment at the end of the day.

We may now proceed to couple the indispensability of the weighting function with Kenneth Arrow's well-known starting point:

> The viewpoint will be taken here that interpersonal comparison of utilities has no meaning and in fact that there is no meaning relevant to welfare comparisons in the measurability of individual utility.
>
> The problem of measuring utility has frequently been compared with the problem of measuring temperature. This comparison is very apt. . . . [D]oes it make sense to say that an increase in temperature from zero degrees to one degree is just as intense as from a hundred degrees to a hundred-and-one degrees. No more can it be said that there is any meaning in

comparing marginal utilities at different levels of well-being.
(1951, 9–10)

A more fundamental problem is presented by the concept of
preference that underlies political and economic theory.
Democracy is in some sense supposed to reflect what people
want. Theorists have refined this to a concept of social preference
and puzzled how it can be determined. We have seen that the concept of utility, wants, or preference is itself not well defined.[98]
How much cloudier is the concept of social preferences! Kenneth
Arrow (1951), John Rawls (1972), and Jon Elster (1989) have tra-
versed the ground. In Elster's words, there is a "large scope of
indeterminacy in social decisions" (1989, 175). But it appears that
these writers and others have viewed preferences as being subjective, as wants in some simple, one-dimensional way.[99] I am suggesting that the indeterminacy is multilayered. Even if preferences, seen subjectively, could be aggregated or reconciled, determining what different members of the populace judge to be the
resulting right political choices creates an indeterminacy of a different order. Put another way, when the public is canvassed for
preferences, is one seeking its wants, values, and goals (with other
considerations set to one side), or is one seeking judgments that
take these personal elements into account *as well as* moral and
political considerations and thus purport to be its best judgments,
all things considered? In tapping preferences we will never know
what we have got. Are the answers raw wants or are they political
positions? At best, differing judgments will drain into different

---

98. Hurley's (1989) extensive treatment of preferences is considered
under "Rationality" in the last chapter.

99. See the earlier discussion under "Practical Reasoning" and Fukuyama's further observation on economic claims: "We readily understand
economic self-interest, but frequently ignore the way it is intimately bound
up with thymotic self-assertion. Higher wages satisfy both the desire for
material things of the desiring part of the soul *and* the desire for the recognition of the thymotic part. In political life, economic claims are seldom
presented as simple demands for more; they are usually couched in terms
of 'economic justice' " (1992, 173).

receptacles to crystallize into political parties and platforms (or result in different responses in a plebiscite) to be accommodated by a variety of democratic systems. But determining social preferences by going *behind* politics appears bankrupt.

Taken together we are left with the conclusion that notwithstanding agreement on a basket of primary values there is an inherent undecidability about second-order social issues and judgments.[100] Such judgments often come with sweeping predictions. A topical example of indeterminacy is given by the fate of the prediction of a future socialist world by Joseph Schumpeter (1950). In spite of the plausibility accorded his views, they have not, a half century later, been borne out. Now we have Fukuyama's converse prediction of the triumph of liberal capitalist democracy. If his prediction is halfway right, the province of judgment will be immeasurably expanded in choosing between the hundred flowers that will bloom, with no conditioned ideological reflex to fall back on. The events of 1989 and their fallout are humbling to prediction.

The consolation of this theoretical indeterminacy is that in spite of theory, experience offers many cases of consensus in small social groups. Indeed, "consensus"—an odd term uniquely applicable to social interaction—captures that indefinable degree of agreement that may fall short of unanimity. There are several things going on here: the judgment of the appropriateness of accepting a consensus rather than a poll, the judgment that a consensus exists, and the avoidance of hard judgments by the canvassed class that would be required by a poll, leaving inner conflicts unresolved. Yet on such foundations many social structures are built. So consensus in large groups may not be much more than the absence of a recalcitrant event such as the loss of an election. Still, tenuous as it is, consensus permits us to take a step back from Elster's (1989) gloom and reflect that while specific policies and social decisions (e.g., the Solomonic decision as to which parent is entitled to custody of a child) are indeterminable,

---

100. Perhaps "third order" is more appropriate to leave room for such generative ideals as autonomy (Hurley) and authenticity (Taylor) which, however, require a lower order of decisions to become operative.

broad directions can occasionally command such limited agreement.

Wide social issues lead to even broader cultural ones. We discussed the challenge thrown to judgment by the onrush of technology that overwhelms simple decision procedures and paradoxically calls on those human faculties beyond technology to assign its products their proper place. There is as well a stream of criticism questioning technological progress, deploring the decay of humanism, rampant consumerism, and urging shifts such as small is beautiful and so forth. How do we assess where we are now against where we were then? The answers should be seen to turn not on a disagreement on any one root value but on the perspective of how good and bad elements are weighed. As post-industrial society ascends the economic curve, issues become ever less quantitative and ever more qualitative—that is, deserving sensitive judgmental treatment. We are used to the power of generative ideas in history. We are less used to recognizing history as the accumulated residue of the way all manner of ideas have been put to use.

In politics there is the inevitable *balancing* between individual liberties, collective (communitarian) goals, and our ideals generally.[101] Isaiah Berlin concludes skeptically:

> But if we are not armed with an *a priori* guarantee of the proposition that a total harmony of true values is somewhere to be found—perhaps in some ideal realm the characteristics of which we can, in our finite state, not so much as conceive—we must fall back on the ordinary resources of empirical observation and ordinary human knowledge. And these certainly give us no warrant for supposing (or even understanding what would be meant by saying) that all good things, or all bad things for that matter, are reconcilable with each other. The world that we encounter in ordinary experience is one in which

---

101. "Balancing" works as a euphemism by suggesting the availability of a readable instrument that masks the severe task each instance calls for. A recurring North American example is offered by the redistribution of electoral boundaries to determine the appropriate deviation from "rep by pop" to satisfy rural and ethnic goals.

we are faced with choices between ends equally ultimate, and claims equally absolute, the realization of some of which must inevitably involve the sacrifice of others.

(1969, 168)

These conflicting claims come to a head in what has been confusingly called the confrontation of positive and negative liberty. Liberty is seen negatively as the absence of constraints[102] (with its well-known qualifications) and positively as the direction by the state toward the fulfillment of some positive ideal. Following Charles Taylor, S. L. Hurley argues that one cannot simply play it safe by shutting the door on positive liberty for fear that a push toward content may lead to mass rule, totalitarianism, and the denial of negative liberty.[103] But while the argument is persuasive that policy must have ideals in the most general sense, it does not follow that the resulting conflicts can be rationally resolved by appeal to some guiding principle. The drab conclusion is rather that by the light of heightened objectivity (where our ideals come in) judgments must be made step-by-step, shifting first this way then that, to maintain the precarious poise to move forward. In all this, judgment enters at every point to separate the constitutional from the political and the political from the private. Elshtain concludes with a singular image:

A central task of political philosophy lies in recognizing, for what it is, what has happened in Europe since 1989. What has happened is the definitive collapse of an attempt to rebuild human society on some overarching *Weltanschauung*. Europe, [Václav] Havel noted, has entered the long tunnel at the end of the light. This is a wonderful metaphor for the democratic drama more generally. There is the light—the glorious light of

---

102. There is an assumption in liberal societies, not beyond empirical refutation, that people free to choose will choose for the best, that they judge rationally. The shift to *autonomy* and *authenticity* dodges this awkward question by the focus on the effects of the process on the inner person.

103. See also Tugendhat, "Liberalism, Liberty and the Issue of Economic Human Rights" (1992, 352).

public freedom, individual liberty, and political equality—and then we move through the long tunnel, a world of politics without end.

(1993, 137)

I would venture beyond Berlin, Elshtain, and, if I understand him right, Nozick, and hazard that the pluralism (a term that perhaps slips too easily into discourse) they recognize as our enduring condition can only be reconciled with objectivity through a radical particularism. As was said earlier, principles are at once too far from and too close to the action to function reliably and freely. They are by definition rigid. At times we find it useful to push them cautiously forward from square to square on an imaginary board until they bump. Yet particular decisions can and, in spite of our logical qualms, do partake of disparate plural elements. And with the acceptance of an overriding commitment to the right ultimate judgment, comes the freedom to indulge in a pluralism of ideals on which we can draw to produce individual judgments that are right.

So, within a cultural tradition large social questions are judgmental, informed not by different values but by how they are prioritized, applied, and shaped to fit particular circumstances. In the post-postmodern world it will increasingly fall to judgment to counter the confusion of multiple presences, the cacophony of voices, the ambivalence of opinions, the secondhandedness of things, to arrive at beliefs held as right. As will be discussed in the next chapter, this assigns to judgment a role in concept formation itself.

V

Cognition and Character

He hath a good judgment that relieth not wholly on his own.
—H. C. Bohn, *Handbook of Proverbs* (1855)

> Men's judgments are
> A parcel of their fortunes; and things outward
> Do draw the inward quality after them,
> To suffer all alike.
> —Shakespeare, *Antony and Cleopatra,* III (c.1606)

Cognition

It is a commonplace to observe that giving the right answer is less important than asking the right question. But at that point conventional wisdom abdicates. What tells us which questions to ask? Presumably *that* question, the answer to which tells us what we want to know. But what tells us what we want to know, what we ought to want to know? Here we come up against a hierarchy of cognitive and noncognitive goals which depends on the twin concepts of importance and appropriateness. The shorthand for this process is judgment. As history has borne out, some simply ask the right questions.

The concept of knowledge itself masks judgmental elements. In *Philosophy and the Mirror of Nature,* Richard Rorty depreciates the semantic concept of knowledge in the sense of his title. Perhaps he goes too far in disabusing us of this image as it relates to stray bits of knowledge such as Vermeer's birth in 1632, where what we know reflects what is the case. At this level the concept of knowledge as a mirror seems apt. There is also an assumption in such an elemental case of the consciousness of knowing that you know. After that scrap of knowledge is acquired consciousness slips away but knowledge is still guaranteed by an operational test, a correct answer to a question. A year or so later, in a different context, you read that Spinoza was born close by in 1632. At what point can it be said that you know that *both* Vermeer and Spinoza were born in 1632?[104] Perhaps it is at the point we put the two birthdates together in our minds as one extended fact. As we saw with belief, this jump from knowledge of one bit of information to knowledge of another is often imposed on a witness by an aggressive counsel in cross-examination: "So witness, you have told us that you knew X, therefore it is clear that you also knew Y, isn't that so?" followed by the lame answer, "I suppose so."

Putting two such elemental facts "together" may of itself not require a judgmental function beyond grouping, but grasping the significance of the conjunction of birthdates, birthplaces, and, ultimately, views of the world, depends upon a range of judgments leading to a composite picture. Bearing it in one's mind is, as Gadamer and Rorty would suggest, not mirror knowledge but *Bildung.*[105] As the

---

104. See Gadamer's (1976, 14) discussion of Aristotle's example of how we come to know the point at which an army stops retreating and stands its ground, in the context of coming to know abstractions generally.

105. See Gadamer's (1992) elaboration of the concept and the later extensive discussion by Rorty (1979) and John McDowell (1994). Rorty considers a translation of *Bildung* as "education," "self-formation," and settles on "edification," which seems high-falutin and too directed to moral improvement to do justice to the implication that a picture is a pic-

German word suggests, there is a pictorial element to the value-tinged fact pattern in the civilized mind. It implies that such a pattern has not been passively received and stamped out but has been forged by an active judgmental function.

Separating out elements is equally critical to cognition. As we saw with the law, we look to judgment to make appropriate distinctions. This becomes apparent in social issues. For example, can the issue of race segregation in schools be distinguished from gender separation in schools? What is said about the role of judg-

---

ture *of* something. Rorty's meaning is captured rather by the adjective *gebildet* (cultivated), one step farther removed from *Bild* (picture) and *bilden* (to fashion or form). Discussing Gadamer's substitution of *Bildung* for knowledge as the goal of thinking, Rorty says (1979, 359–60):

> From the educational, as opposed to the epistemological or the technological, point of view, the way things are said is more important than the possession of truths. . . .
>
> The contrast between the desire for edification and the desire for truth is, for Gadamer, not an expression of a tension which needs to be resolved or compromised. If there is a conflict, it is between the Platonic-Aristotelian view that the *only* way to be edified is to know what is out there (to reflect the facts accurately—to realize our essence by knowing essences) and the view that the quest for truth is just one among many ways in which we might be edified.

This leaves the field wide open for judgment. Perhaps too wide. For, while where alternatives and choice enter, judgment enters as well, such choice is at a minimum where we are confronted by the bulk of our experience. Were it otherwise, we would not share it. At this level the image of the mirror holds. But as knowledge and its objects become attenuated, choice, ways of putting things, and thus judgment, enter ever more. Between these two there is an intractable tension (reflected in realist and antirealist positions) that cannot be released by appeal to edification. Rather than a notion of self-improvement, I would draw on the overtones of *Bildung* as a composite, judgment-created picture in the service of a wider, deeper knowledge. For contrary to Rorty, Gadamer, and possibly Taylor, the view here put forward is that the necessary, but perhaps not sufficient, way to edification is to know what is out there.

ment in incorporating or distinguishing atomic facts to constitute knowledge or *Bildung* is magnified in the social sciences. In this domain general statements and predictions must pass through the unpredictable territory of individual human decisions. Economic forecasting is a case in point. Chaos theory and fuzzy logic attempt to deal with the randomness of human decisions and the messy way we draw our inferences. Individual decisions, like the single beat of a butterfly's wings, are unpredictable yet have the potential to create tempests.

The dependence of the social sciences on judgmental factors is due not only to the issues of composition and distinction but as well to the problem of characterization systemic of taxonomy. In psychology we observe a certain character trait. What scale is to be used to label it and where on that scale of its potential should an individual's trait be placed? The problem is acute with respect to self-assessment and self-knowledge. What scale did Socrates have in mind? Characteristics such as "bright," "ambitious," "honest," "selfish," point two ways. Once a scale is selected and the place on the scale identified in relation to a standard of normalcy, does one look up or down? Measurement and significance overlap. This brings home the inevitable place in the social sciences of comparisons (odious only if inappropriate), the appropriateness of the scale employed, and the significance of the determination, all tied to a judgmental function. In the preceding chapter we examined these considerations on economic and political theory.

I have talked loosely of facts and observation. As Jerry Fodor has pointed out (see footnote 136), computer-run experiments do not result, except in a contrived way, in observations but in *data*. The old empirical anchor of observation has been hoisted to leave us adrift to make sense of the data. As empiricism is seen to be less and less beholden to observation, the more a judgmental function will be recognized as critical to carry the cognitive process forward. Max Black quotes (1954, 190) C. D. Broad's dictum "induction is the glory of Science" but "the scandal of Philosophy." A scandal because not justifiable by some formal canon. The scandal is dissipated if we see induction as simply the most common example of judgment and hence justifiable itself and in its applications to the same extent.

These considerations return us to a pervasive methodological issue: the judgmental function to apply generalizations and abstractions to particular events.[106] As was noted earlier, at a deep level the application of simple properties such as "red" or categories of objects such as "chair" have been said to involve a judgmental function. For the later Berkeley judgment was a critical part of cognition. The senses themselves know nothing. Knowledge does not adhere in perception but is added to perception by the judicial department of the mind. This pushes the case for judgment too far. While we hesitate to call perceptions of red chairs judgments, as we saw in the discussion on the application of rules, the judgmental function becomes evident in determining borderline applications.

In matters relating to human conduct and morality, recourse to the particular in practical wisdom is emphasized by Aristotle:

> But let this point be first thoroughly understood between us, that all which can be said on moral action must be said in outline, as it were, and not exactly: for as we remarked at the commencement, such reasoning only must be required as the nature of the subject-matter admits of, and matters of moral action and expediency have no fixedness any more than matters of health. And if the subject in its general maxims is such, still less in its application to particular cases is exactness obtainable: because these fall not under any art or system of rules, but it must be left in each instance to the individual agents to look to the exigencies of the particular case, as it is in the art of healing, or that of navigating a ship. (*Ethics* II. 1104a, trans. D. P. Chase [London: Dent, Everyman ed., 1942], p. 28)

> Nor again does practical wisdom consist in a knowledge of general principles only, but it is necessary that one should know also the particular details, because . . . action is con-

---

106. Here and throughout I use "particular" mainly in an adjectival, nontechnical sense. See Michael Dummett's (1973, 471) account of the replacement of the pre-Fregean duality of universal/particular by the logical concept of *object*.

cerned with details: for which reason sometimes men who
have not much knowledge are more practical than others who
have. . . . Since then Practical Wisdom is apt to act, one ought
to have both kinds of knowledge, or, if only one, the knowledge of details rather than of Principles. (*Ethics* VI.1141b
[Ibid., p. 139])

The judgmental function required to apply abstractions to
particular events is coupled with the difficulty of characterizing
the phenomena that are the objects of cognition. Here we move
in the opposite direction from the particular to the general and
abstract. To make sense of particulars, to assess them, to characterize them, we turn to judgment. There is incessant movement
back and forth between particulars and abstractions and between
levels of abstraction. Thought and language demand it. Much is
unconscious, much is indistinct, but some is watched over, cen-
sored, judgmental.

Characterization becomes acute in the most theoretical realms
of knowledge. Niels Bohr gives the example of the wave and particle explanations of light for his theory of complementary aspects
of reality which cannot be contradicted empirically. The microbi-
ologist Guenther Stent[107] has adopted a similar notion to account
for physicalist and moral explanations of mental states in his
account of free will. He concludes from what was previously said
about the limitations of predictability and the crumbling of the old
determinacy:

Admittedly, a natural world such as that envisaged in the late
eighteenth century by Laplace—where events are totally determined by initial conditions, from the beginning to the end of
time—could hardly provide scope for the exercise of free will.
But, as it turns out, our actual natural world is not Laplacean.
Rather, it is largely *indeterminate,* its events being subject to
microphysical (i.e., quantum mechanical) or macrophysical
(i.e., "chaotic") contingencies—I mean here that although the
person's will is by no means immune to causal influence by the

---

107. Guenther Stent, "Can We Explain the Mind?" *Encounter* (March
1990).

natural world, there does remain a residue of independence from such causal influence. By virtue of this residue, the person's rational faculty is the final arbiter of what is actually being willed. The outcome of this autonomous arbitration process is not capricious or random, but determined by the soul.

What Stent says can be put less grandly by substituting for *rational faculty* and *free will* the more pedestrian but more comprehensive faculty of judgment. The *arbitration* process, while not necessarily as autonomous as Stent believes, governs not only our moral beliefs and actions but our intellectual lives as well.

There is a connection here to Davidson's theory of anomalous monism:[108] there are no strict determinative laws on the basis of which mental events can be predicted. This appears to have the profound consequence that human conduct which is habitually explainable in our everyday vocabulary of mental events, but not in a neurophysicalist vocabulary, is theoretically undetermined. Therefore the social sciences that rest on human conduct which lead back to such events are implicated accordingly. Prediction in these sciences can proceed in two ways. One is to trace the specific causal chain which will inevitably lead to the ultimate nexus of human conduct, itself the result of impenetrable variables. The other horn, statistics, assumes parallel circumstances which cannot be assumed to be so because the relevant mental processes

---

108. Davidson (1980, 253) believes that the same mental event can have a psychological description and a physical description. The physical description will never be able to predict the event described psychologically. That is the anomalous part. But he sticks to the monism because he holds there is only one event being described which belongs to the rest of the physical universe. The reasoning rests on the assumption that the same event can be described differently. The example given is Brutus *killing* Caesar and Brutus *stabbing* Caesar. Here, though, we know at the outset *what the event is*. We can thus describe it differently by attending to different aspects. But with mental/physical events this is the very thing we don't know. For an approach from the other side of the river see Weiskrantz (ed.), *Thought without Language* (1988), a collection of papers on the right cerebral hemisphere, that is more about thinking than thought, and "Thinking" by Holyoak and Spellman (1993).

cannot be identified. So we have come full circle. Instead of action being predictable in theory but not predictable in practice, we now have action unpredictable in theory but clearly, within limits, predictable in practice.

The discussion of the appropriateness of certain vocabularies to describe certain classes of events leads to the consideration of the appropriate level of explanation with respect to a particular subject. Considerations of what is the appropriate level of explanation has a well-known parallel, going back at least to Aristotle, in identifying the cause of an event, say a traffic accident. Was the cause of the pedestrian's death the impact of the skull on the pavement, the failure of the car's brakes, the failure to have the brakes repaired, the poor street lighting, and so on? While we can say that these are all causes we dilute the usefulness of the concept accordingly. Clearly the answer lies in giving an appropriate explanation of the event, appropriate to answer a more precise question. All theoretical discussions are bedeviled by the problem of determining the appropriate level of explanation and by the unavailability of any other criterion except retreat to the question asked. W. V. Quine puts the example of behaviorism as useful at a certain level to demonstrate instructive regularities.[109] And in philosophy the debate has moved from the place of language to the relationship of levels of language.

This leads to a look at explanatory models. What, after all, is a paradigm shift but a judgment that another conceptual model is more appropriate? I am, of course, by casting light on judgment suggesting just such a shift to it from a range of other concepts. And where does knowledge stop and speculation begin, or perhaps the other way around? Take the fascination with the extrapolation of the concept of entropy nestling innocently in the Second Law of Thermodynamics:

---

109. It is ironic that it was Quine's technical arguments that led to the dissolution of the analytic/synthetic distinction and thus away from positivism to a pragmatic view of how language works. Yet pragmatic reasons continue to justify the distinction at certain levels. As I have argued (1989), it may be Hart's modified positivist view of law rather than, say, interpretation, which best accounts for the courtroom phenomena that want explaining.

Any process that converts energy from one form to another must lose some as heat. Perfect efficiency is impossible. The universe is a one-way street. *Entropy must always increase in the universe and in any hypothetical isolated system within it.* However expressed, the Second Law is a rule from which there seems no appeal. In thermodynamics that is true. But the Second Law has had a life of its own in intellectual realms far removed from science, taking the blame for disintegration of societies, economic decay, the breakdown of manners, and many other variations on the decadent theme.

(Gleick 1987, 308)

Stephen Hawking sees entropy as "order becoming disorder" (1988, 103, 152) as one of the three governing cosmological principles. To the extent such everyday expressions are applicable at all, perhaps "structure" is more apt than "order." But how far can one take either one of these concepts? Cannot humankind (indeed, life itself) be seen not merely as a great back eddy in the disordering of the cosmic flow, but as a falsifying phenomenon? After all, if, as Hawking admits, we are committed willy-nilly to an anthropic view, are we not entitled to *weight* the increase in structure/order from one new bit of knowledge differently from its loss due to the exhalation of our breath?[110]

While we may help ourselves liberally to such speculation, the required critical judgment brings in considerations of importance and appropriateness. A similar issue revolves around the objectivity of historical generalizations. Here is E. H. Carr:

The historian, too, in his task of interpretation needs his standard of significance, which is also his standard of objectivity, in order to distinguish between the significant and the accidental; and he too can find it only in relevance to his end in view. But this is necessarily an evolving end, since the evolving interpretation of the past is a necessary function of history.

(1990, 120–21)

---

110. As Ruskin says, "No weight nor mass nor beauty of execution can outweigh one grain or fragment of thought" (quoted in the preface to the first edition of the poems of Emily Dickinson [1890] by Thomas Wentworth Higginson).

This questioning of objectivity in history has been taken much further by postmodernist writers. One no longer discovers continents, one *invents* America, the Middle Ages, Quebec.[111] It is tempting to overblow this skepticism. Is there not a vast body of historical fact and indeed textual interpretation on which all historians could agree? Although wildly impractical, there is nothing in theory to preclude the construction of such a body to see just how much consensus exists irrespective of ideology and ethnic origins. After all, if there is consensus on other aspects of reality, why can there not be limited consensus on that part of reality composed of the past?[112] With respect to the year 1492, there will be a residue of agreement on some matters and disagreement on others.[113] How does the Holocaust differ? The point is not to deny the place of "interpretation" in history but that judgment is required to resolve its proper place and weight.

This brings me to question the use of *interpretation* in this context and thus to return to the distinction between judgment and interpretation. It is perhaps not excessive to say that writers have hijacked interpretation from its settled use to mean too

---

111. See A. Sherratt "The Fabrication of the Past," *Times Literary Supplement,* October 21, 1994.

112. Prediction from history is in theory no different from other prediction. After all, all facts used as information are past facts. It is not the past that is the problem but our inability to isolate and align the few appropriate and essential facts to support a prediction. There are too many lessons to know which not to repeat. History may tell us that a populace hates tyrants, but it also tells us that you cannot predict if and when a tyranny will be overthrown. The *Wall Street Journal* (July 20, 1994) reports the views of seven investment professionals who each see different historical precedents to the then market conditions. See Dummett's (1978) "The Reality of the Past" and "Bringing about the Past" and Toulmin (1972, 491).

113. Tversky and Kahneman (1981) compare the effect the linguistic framing of choices has on preferences to the veridical framing of views of a mountain has on estimates of heights. They recognize the critical difference that in veridical disagreement one can appeal to outside measurement. So perhaps with history. Some answers are provided by the fortuitous appeal to dates. As Barbara Tuchman observed, dates establish sequences—what preceded, what followed—the beginning of determining causal connections.

much and sometimes very little. After all, the paradigm case of language, when it works as it ought, is precisely when it doesn't need interpretation, when it is transparent, not in the sense of seeing something on the other side but in the sense of the language (and even the consciousness of understanding it) being itself unseen. Writers who maintain that we are always interpreting when listening or reading are not fair to the social facts; the word loses its point. It is only when language fails or is put to special use that meaning, and hence interpretation, comes into the picture. The distinction between interpretation and judgment is also seen in noting that judgments are always *decisive* in a way which interpretations are not. Indeed, for those who plump for interpretation as all-pervasive and hence unconscious, they could not be so. Interpretation hovers somewhere between unselfconscious understanding (which is affected by all sorts of things) and judgment, which is a decision that may on occasion be made to attribute a certain meaning to a text.

Most counterexamples can be explained away. A diner at the next table is overheard to ask, "What do you mean?" The question has nothing to do with misunderstanding what was said, of interpreting the language. The questioner wants to know further thoughts behind the understood utterance—the motive, implications, agenda of the companion. What is wanted is to know *more,* different things. Again, interpreting a statute is a term of art that refers to determining (making a judgment) what the law is on the application of its provisions to the case at hand. Interpreting a play or poem (an example of special use) can mean all manner of things: determining all the things the author had in mind, ideas suggested by the text regardless of what the author had in mind, or any of dozens of elaborate options found in the literature. The issue is not what is meant generically by interpreting a poem but rather our making a preliminary judgment as to what we want the phrase "interpreting a poem" to mean, what is cognitively appropriate. Once determined, we can move directly to the task and the concept of interpretation drops out.

So we are left with interpretation confined to foreign translation and to domestic puzzlement. An example of the latter is given by Davidson:

> If you see a ketch sailing by and your companion says, "Look at that handsome yawl," you may be faced with a problem of interpretation. One natural possibility is that your friend has mistaken a ketch for a yawl and has formed a false belief. But if his vision is good and his line of sight favourable it is even more plausible that he does not use the word "yawl" quite as you do, and has made no mistake about the position of the jigger on the passing yacht.
>
> (1984, 196)

But while this example shows us the glue between meaning and belief, it also indicates that such radical interpretation at the roots of communication comes to the surface only where language fails at the margins. Interpretation in this traditional sense is a process of getting clear about difficult language. What meaning does the group of words point to. Whether meanings are "there" to be pointed to or not, the way we use "interpretation" assumes they are. Judgment, on the other hand, is not about language but about issues—thoughts and ideas—including only occasionally deciding about meanings. Writers have been side-tracked by the canard of interpretation from dealing with judgment by this and other confusions. What they lump under interpretation, on examination collapses into three different categories. One is the straightforward process of clarifying meaning-puzzles, the second is making judgments. The third residual category is mistaking nonproblematic understanding for interpretation.[114] To confound the last two is to mistake a result (or more

---

114. Douglas Hofstadter (1980, 165, 582) attributes his intuition that meaning is to be found in the text or meaningful object, to the predictability that over time most people will "pull out" the same meaning from them. Pulling out the meaning, or form, does not involve a decision procedure or judgment. The *syntactic* aspects of form can be read off. But the *semantic* aspects of form are, however, not confined to the text or art object. "Meanings—both musical and linguistic—are to some extent localizable, to some extent spread around. . . . We can say that musical pieces and pieces of text are triggers, and partly carriers of explicit meaning" (p. 583). We should note that what is triggered outside the text or object, where interpretation is required, while not definable and open-ended, is nonetheless *out there* to be "searched out" and "integrated with preexistent information" and not imposed on the text or object by the interpreter.

neutrally, a given) for a process. It is to impute an inevitable process of interpreting behind every act of understanding, which Wittgenstein thought to be an impregnable dead end. One can speculate on what lies behind mere understanding, but to take whatever one finds there as the process that constitutes interpretation or, indeed, judgment, is a confusion of levels. How the thoughts and ideas with which judgment deals are themselves hostage to language is a daunting problem largely beyond this book. But I would hazard that how our minds work precludes transitivity between the two sets of processes or relations. There are no shortcuts to considering them separately.[115]

---

115. Traditionally, those who argue for the sanctity of objectivity and truth do so from positing the reality of prior concepts which truth finds, discovers, or reflects. Approached from the other direction, we might say, if our minds are committed to the elemental concepts of objectivity and truth, then we are also committed to concepts that stand behind interpretation. A provocative example is provided by the gay/lesbian community's campaign to replace reference in the media to their "special" rights with "civil" rights, "agenda" with "goals," "preference" with "orientation." For the professedly fair-minded there is here no refuge in language and interpretation from wrestling to arrive at the *right* thought. Another more erudite example is given by indirect quotation, as has been done by Davidson (1984), McFetridge (1975), and Rumfitt (1993). For "Galileo said that the earth moves" is true whether he muttered (if he did) "Eppur se muove" or "Se muove la terra" or to a passing Englishman, "The earth, she moves." We cannot (*pace* Quine and Rorty) do without the "idea" idea. Once there, we need deal with them, indeed must, as with less lasting things. And thoughts can be seen as structured ideas, which gives plausibility to the practice of translating Frege's "thoughts" as "propositions." I take McDowell's (1994) "space of reasons" to occupy roughly this realm of ideas, thoughts, concepts, and meanings. He comes at the abiding puzzle of *Mind and World* crossways. He sees a divide between nature (and its laws) and this "space" (and its spontaneity), which he struggles to dissolve by naturalizing a "spooky" platonism. But is not nature-and-its-laws itself in the meaning camp? And can we not accept this space as the strangest product of nature just because it resists reduction and remains *sui generis*? While John Searle (1994) convincingly rescues consciousness (thinking, etc.) as a *sui generis* product of nature, he stops short of delineating *its* products in turn as *sui generis*.

We saw that judgments are put forward as being right and are themselves judged by us as right or wrong. Interpretations, on the other hand, can only be so classed if we are already waiting with a defined background of meaning against which the interpretation can be matched. A quite different use is revealed by the common question, "What interpretation do *you* put on it?" Here interpretation works in the language like *preference,* discussed later, where the questioner looks for subjective input that may be described as interesting or original but to which external confirmation is inappropriate.

Once the epistemological debris surrounding interpretation has been cleared, the issue left open is a moral one. Given that we inevitably come to a text differently from the author regardless of time and place, and given further that we can never be certain of the writer's intentions, do we nonetheless have a duty to attempt as best we can to determine the writer's intent, her meaning, to see the text as she saw it, and even more so, not to distort it? From this special case we pass easily to the everyday speech of others.

Returning from this digression on interpretation, we note another distinction that needs comment. There is a natural inclination to contrast the role of judgment in cognition with its role in matters relating to value. While I previously indicated the connection between our fundamental values and our recognitions of importance and therefore judgment, I have stayed clear of discussing moral judgments as such although they constitute our most profound choices. The emphasis on judgment as a type of choice approaches the position of the existentialist in the moral sphere. These choices, what leads up to them and the commitment that follows, are logically central to moral phenomena, although the frequency of such choices has been much exaggerated. For the mere *holding* of a value does not constitute a judgment. It is the considered decision to hold a value that is the judgment. And it is the complaint of the moralist that we come by too many of our values uncritically, without judgment.

We need also distinguish between holding these fundamental values from the process of *evaluation* which was discussed briefly in connection with art criticism. Because evaluation revolves round values it has been thought to be outside the cognitive realm. But by and large evaluation reduces to description, as does cognition. Take the mundane case of setting salaries, or the allocation of bonuses, or what is close to home, setting compensation levels among professional partners. The task requires the evaluation of the individual in question, that is, a description of a person's conduct and potential in terms of given categories or criteria. Into which category does the person fit? This matching between the description of the person and the characteristics of the category cannot be accomplished mechanically. The process casts light on the judgmental elements inherent in description generally and hence on cognition. Most moral judgments of persons or actions are descriptive in this way and most disputes turn on the validity of the descriptions of particular situations rather than on disagreements on the moral values themselves.

These considerations of the role of judgment in cognition return us to an Aristotelian emphasis on the gritty particular, the particular event, the particular circumstance, the particular question, the particular decision. Perhaps Kant's use of the seemingly gratuitous prefix, judgment, in the first *Critique* did spring from a recognition that statements must be transformed through a pragmatic commitment (judgment) to deserve cognitive legitimacy. That is, the cognitive task has not been completed until a commitment has been made to apply the generalization, abstraction, concept, universal to the event (the specific belief), a commitment which can only be discharged by doing it. Knowing a law or rule generally can be seen as a loftier but softer kind of knowledge than knowing how it applies to a certain event. Abstractions must be capable of being turned to particular account. Problems of qualification that plague general statements of value shrink the more narrowly they are framed until they reduce to a particular act or object, at which point they tend to dissipate. It is judgment that gets us to that point. Similarly, the hullabaloo surrounding relativism dies down the closer we approach a specific application. Differences may remain, but to account for them by appeal to relativism is off-base. It is the inescapable recourse to the particular that cuts across Aristotle's distinction, hardened into dogma, between practical wisdom (know-how) and knowledge. There is not scientific knowledge and other kinds, there is only knowledge differently derived, eliciting different expectations. So judgment works on the insights of intelligence and imagination to put them to use. Without it (except when seen as art) such insights wither or misfire. In this sense philosophical theories, to the extent they do not help to clarify particular lower-level problems, may rightly take refuge in aesthetic justification.

How is the potential diversity of judgments to be squared with a shared view of the world which we by and large accept? There is always the transcendental judgment waiting in the back of our minds: how much faith to place in our own ultimate judgment. It is the old riddle of the possibility of knowledge, seen in the light of the judgmental function. What suggests itself is that through our common natures and a sufficiently common fund of essential experiences, we come to make sufficiently common judgments to arrive at sufficiently common views of reality.[116] This communality answers the question put by Wallace Stevens,

---

116. Can this view of one reality be stretched to cover moral values? One account would go something like this. Earlier I had spoken of tolerance for values of others, which implied differences. But these values are on the outer shell. When we consider the deep ones, it may help to invoke the image of moral values as a special sort of legislation from which the legislator has vanished. The point is that asking who is the legislator is quite different from asking what is the legislation. For it is clearly *there.* Those that are devoid of the sense to detect it are treated as pathological. To borrow an example from Gilbert Harman (1977), we recognize in a flash that setting a cat on fire (except in extraordinary circumstances) is wrong. The second point of the legislation analogy is the fact that *it is in place,* much as the criminal code or a municipal parking regulation. That being so, it doesn't make sense to ask whether the parking regulation is "objective" or not. Neither whether our deep values are.

One can ask whether something else under different conditions could have been enacted, which leads back to two issues which I passed by: what is special about moral rules and who is the legislator? To take the second question first, there are many candidates: God, genetic wiring, evolution, our cultural history, intersubjectivity. The odd thing is that, possibly

> Twenty men crossing a bridge
> Into a village,
> Are twenty men crossing twenty bridges,
> Into twenty villages,
> Or one man
> Crossing a single bridge into a village.
>
> ("Metaphors of a Magnifico")

Yet there hangs an epistemological cloud with metaphysical fallout:

> Kick at the rock Sam Johnson, break your bones:
> But cloudy, cloudy is the stuff of stones.
>
> We milk the cow of the world, and as we do
> We whisper in her ear, "You are not true."
>
> (Richard Wilbur, "Epistemology")

---

because the analysis is in reverse, assumptions on different candidates yield the same answer. Even differing cultural histories. We will never believe that if another society holds that the gratuitous burning of a cat is good that it is using "good" in the same way we do. We will never shake our belief that it is morally wrong, which goes a long way to answering our first question on the distinctiveness of moral rules. It is open to us to ask if a legal or other rule is morally good but not whether a moral one is. Agreement on the meaning of "morally good" (as of "truth") is inextricably bound up with agreement on its use in defining cases. If someone agrees that 2 plus 2 equals 4 but disagrees that the statement is true, you have a meaning problem. It may of course be that the unknown legislator is silently at work so that in another age "we" will differ. But then we may not see that wall *as* red either. See Marcia Cavell's (1993, 110) discussion of infants not seeing a red ball *as* red.

Because this account may fail to convince with respect to shallower judgments, it suggests a discontinuity between them and the deeper ones to which perhaps "moral" should be restricted. We may need to accept that there is no clear cutoff. Of more concern is that the conduct of cat burners and bombers suggests there is no sealed border between judgment directed behavior and dysfunctional behavior. Something has gone wrong in the mechanism that forms the beliefs and values that drives such conduct. In that sense, extremist "crazies" are just that. That is not to say that they escape responsibility. But with them judgment has no purchase.

In the last paragraph of his book Hao Wang (1986), following his discussion of Kant, fastens on two elements:

> The slogan "reverence for what we know" sounds bland and negative. How do we reach what we know? It is, first of all, necessary to single out what is *essential* from the vast domain of what the human species knows today. And then, how do we use the data in an *appropriate* way? [Emphasis mine]

That *importance* and *appropriateness* are central to cognition is not surprising if one thinks of knowledge itself as a perception of the object's relations. How do the relevant salient features of the object fit the relevant salient features of other relevant salient things? So, bits of knowledge can in theory be atomized into perceptions of importance and fit. *In theory,* because in fact knowledge comes to us discretely where few of these relations show. This realist view need not be seen as inconsistent with the relational position. It is rather of a piece with the wave/particle duality.[117] We need reconcile ourselves to oscillate between them. As we ascend, knowledge becomes ever more the answer to questions asked and thus hostage to them. The analogue to our aim on the abstract level for knowledge or *Bildung* is, with respect to particular decisions, to deserve trust for our individual judgments. It is the crossover we recognize as wisdom.

Artificial Judgment

From what has been said about the place of judgment in cognition it is natural to wonder about the potential of judgment by computer. "Intelligence" in the artificial intelligence literature covers a grab bag of mental processes, for it is the aim of the AI program to simulate the most comprehensive workings of the mind. Yet it is one of my arguments that it is doing a disservice to understanding the cognitive function not to separate out various subfunctions of comprehension, reasoning, imagination, and judgment. Ironically, light is

---

117. See Putnam (1991) in his extensive treatment of this issue.

shed on the usefulness of these distinctions by observing the degrees of progress or its absence made in simulating such functions in AI. It is no surprise that the greatest progress has been made with respect to deductive inference and computational procedures. For computers (also called universal Turing machines after the theorist Alan Turing) are in theory capable of manipulating any formal system far better than the human brain. As Paul Churchland puts it,

> The interesting thing about a universal Turing machine is that, for any well defined computational procedures whatever, a universal Turing machine is capable of simulating the machine that will execute those procedures. . . . The important question is whether the activities that constitute conscious intelligence are all computational procedures of some kind or other. The guiding assumption of AI is that they are, and its aim is to construct actual programs that will simulate them.
>
> (1990, 105)

But when we come to examining how far this program has succeeded with another fundamental cognitive process, inductive inference, we note that the results have been lackluster. Hilary Putnam (1988) has summarized a number of the seemingly insuperable obstacles faced by computers with problems of induction. There is first the ability to recognize similarities discussed previously. He points out that in the interesting cases physical similarities are not definable but require the attribution of purposes to agents. He gives the example of a computer determining whether a particular object is a knife. This difficulty is compounded where the similarities are expressed by adjectives and verbs rather than by nouns. Take white. What has the skin pigment of Caucasians in common with a sheet of paper?[118]

---

118. A related challenge arises in the indexing of the vast databanks made available by computers. Without being able to access a particular facet of the data relevant to the searcher, the prodigious memory is useless. How to characterize just that matching aspect without an endless regress of indexing? Programmers are now moving from a fixed index to an adaptive pattern recognition mechanism intended to mimic the brain, giving a hint as to what may underlie intelligence, imagination, and judgment.

A major problem derives from what has been described as the existence of conflicting inductions. Putnam repeats the example given by Nelson Goodman that we know no Inuit speaker has ever entered Emerson Hall at Harvard. But could we predict that an Alaskan Ukluk would stop speaking Inuit if he entered Emerson Hall? The reason the induction fails here is because of the better entrenched inductively supported law that people don't lose their ability to speak a language upon entering a new place. But the point is how do we know which rule governs? AI researchers reply that the hope is to feed sufficient *background* knowledge into the memory. But this wouldn't be sufficient. Algorithms would have to be devised to manipulate the information to give the results our minds would otherwise arrive at. The root problem is to select the right bit of background knowledge. Marvin Minsky (1985) attempts a solution to this problem of the selection of background knowledge by postulating the idea of language frames.[119] "A child reads: Mary was invited to Jack's party. She wondered whether he would like a kite." Minsky (1985, 261) calls it common sense for the child to realize that the kite would be a birthday present. He attributes the knowledge to previous experience which he pictures as a "party invitation frame."[120]

---

119. This use of a frame here is opposite to the one for art objects. It is a commonplace to note that to make an art object of something is to frame it. In that case the function of the frame is not to include a field of context but to exclude the context to define the object. The frame is definitional. The fiat is imposed by the artist as it is by the courts in interpreting statutes dealing with tax and regulatory matters. Is a vitamin a "drug" or a "food"? Does a time charterer "operate" a ship or does building a logging road constitute "logging"? In constitutional law the doctrine of *pith and substance* sprang up. Is provincial legislation regulating hours of work of pipeline workers in pith and substance "labor legislation" or "pipeline legislation" and thus *ultra vires* the province? We are back with the *importance* bundle of concepts.

120. Some critics have seen the frame problem as intractable. Not so Lormond (1990) who pooh-poohs the objections by Dennet, and Fodor. See also Searle (1994).

I argue the problems Putnam sees with AI induction can be attributed to the presence of judgmental processes as indispensable to induction. These judgmental elements appear in their pure form in explicit exercises of judgment. To the extent that part of that process involves computations of probabilities, the tracing of sequential chains of deductive arguments and decision trees, computers can play a large role. But the quintessential elements of judgment, recognitions of importance, and appropriateness do not themselves appear capable of formalization.[121] There is no further rule to formulate. A trivial example of the inability of computers to differentiate degrees of importance and relevance, despite the diligent efforts of programmers, is brought home by the financial statements churned out by accounting firms and financial institutions. The root of our aversion to such computer-generated statements is the effort required to extract the relevant and significant from the extraneous and confusing. Information overload signals a failure to determine importance and appropriateness.

But perhaps the most intriguing ground for AI skepticism is the assumption of the mind as Grand Program. Putnam invokes the authority of François Jacob:

> Evolution should not, Jacob wrote, be thought of as a designer who sits down and produces a lovely blueprint and then constructs organisms according to the blueprint. Evolution should rather be thought of as a tinker with a shop full of spare parts, interesting "junk," etc. [*bricolage*]. Every so often the tinker gets an idea: "I wonder if it would work if I tried using this bicycle wheel in that doohickey?" Many of the tinker's bright ideas fail, but every so often one works. The result is organisms with many arbitrary features as well as serendipitous ones.

---

121. Note, however, the attempt to design ever more sophisticated computer systems to help lawyers search for legal precedents. It is claimed for the University of British Columbia's FLEXICON program: "The final result is then displayed on the computer screen as a 'search profile' which lists each *appropriate* legal authority ranked in order of its relevance" (*The Lawyers Weekly,* October 25, 1991; emphasis mine).

Now, imagine that the tinker becomes a programmer. Still thinking like a tinker, he develops "natural intelligence," not by writing a Grand Program and then building a device to realize it but by introducing one device or programming idea after another. . . . The net result could be that natural intelligence is not the expression of some *one* program but the expression of billions of bits of "tinkering."

(Putnam 1988, 272)

Admittedly, some judgmental elements may be formalized although Roger Penrose (1994) argues that even mathematics eludes the net of computability. But it will remain systematically impossible that questions of importance and appropriateness in archetypal situations will ever be resolved by computers.[122] I borrow a remarkable quotation from Descartes given by Daniel Dennett (1988, 284):

It is indeed conceivable that a machine could be made so that it would utter words, and even words appropriate to the presence of physical acts or objects which cause some change in its origins; as, for example, if it was touched in some spot that it would ask what you wanted to say to it; if in another, that it would cry that it was hurt, and so on for similar things. But it could never modify its phrases to reply to the sense of whatever was said in its presence, as even the most stupid men can do.

"To modify its phrases to reply" captures the essence of the judgmental function which computers can't but "even the most stupid men can do." Computers may think but even a stupid man can do what a computer can't, *judge*.

There is also this. Electronics implies simultaneity. Being on-

---

122. It could be argued against me that it is precisely those cognitive functions which at any given time have not yet been reduced to computerization that are labeled judgmental. Douglas Hofstadter hints at such a position (1980). Since 1980 much software has been written to perform lower management function. But as computer booster Richard A. Shaffer concludes (*Forbes,* January 30, 1995): "Let's be realistic. Computer programs aren't going to replace the judgment in business management."

line gives horizontal reach now. But being wired into a computer grid denies the depth of process. What flashes on is not a decision, even less a judgment. It is perhaps an answer but one to which the concepts of objectivity, fallibility, and process are foreign. Once an algorithm, always an algorithm, which merits the retort, "But that's not a judgment." In such a world judgment disappears.

Character

I hope that a line, however crooked, has been seen to run through the quotations on judgment appearing at the beginning of each chapter. All recognize it as a profound part of our nature. All ring true in their own way. The writers have in effect treated judgment as a discrete faculty. I see no harm in rehabilitating the concept of *faculty* as a convenient label to designate a bundle of mental processes that at the level of common usage present a unitary face to the outside observer. In this sense intelligence, in the IQ sense, whatever its complex components, can usefully be referred to as a faculty. In the same sense I suggest it is useful to think of judgment as a faculty. Two necessary sticks in the bundle are the ability to identify what is essential and what is appropriate. With respect to any particular matter we would not say that someone had judgment if he could not identify the important issues or what was appropriate in the circumstances. A third stick is a commitment to objectivity. Grafted on may be a special skill related to a particular field, of developing an eye and nose for its important and appropriate features.

The question arises whether this capacity for judgment is, within limits, transferable to different fields, whether it operates across different domains. While this remains a subject for empirical investigation, it is clear from English usage that by attributing good judgment to another we usually do so without qualification as to a specific area, which in itself implies confidence in a certain breadth of application. It is a fact of our experience that we regard certain persons as having good judgment over a wide domain, wider than our own evidence of their past experience would otherwise warrant. Often our inferences are justified. But while this seems clear where such disparate areas are nonspecialist, it is intriguing to speculate whether the person who exercises good judgment as a lawyer would have good judgment as a doctor if he had chosen the other profession.

Such a judgmental capacity is intertwined with character. The link between judgment and character is acknowledged somewhat surprisingly by Frege:

> We are probably best in accord with ordinary usage if we take a judgement to be an act of judging, as a leap is an act of leaping. . . . With an act there also belongs an agent, and we do not know the act completely if we do not *know the agent*.[123] [Emphasis mine]

We see this link when considering objectivity, which implies a self-confident, integrated personality that does not permit ulterior motives to intrude into the judgment. Objectivity requires an inner strength to be honest with oneself. Personality disorders are likely to lead to bad judgment, not only in the area related to the disorder but to judgments generally. The causal chain also holds the other way. A proper estimate (judgment) of self-worth is the foundation of emotional stability. Yet where is the capacity to judge more critical and the markers less visible? How do we make the one-to-one correspondence between terms like "honesty" and what's inside? If judgment is quintessentially human, one consequence is that it is not easy for hardware and software to replicate. Another is, however, that it comes laden with the baggage of its human condition.

The judgmental qualities of discrimination and discretion are intellectual as well as character traits.[124] The mark of intellectual sophistication, and more generally of all cognition, is discrimina-

---

123. As quoted by Bell (1987); also see Burge (1992).

124. Discrimination as judgment is seen in the Latin root in Hannah Arendt's (1978, 263) reference to Cicero's *On the Orator*: "For everybody discriminates (*diiudicare*), distinguishes between right and wrong in matters of art and proportion by some silent sense without any knowledge of art and proportion."

tion. It is another aspect of the ability to fit events and ideas into categories. There is an overlap here with intelligence seen as pattern recognition. One must be able to "see" the relevant distinction. It requires a mental acuity of vision parallel to the art critic who can spot a fake Etruscan bronze ten paces away. Discrimination is essential to determining relevance, importance, and therefore judgment. Yet judgment is also essential to discrimination in isolating the features to attend to. As a personality trait in the moral domain, discrimination is equally important. So Epictetus held that our paramount moral concern was to discriminate between things that are in our power and things not in our power.

Robert Browning dramatizes the want of discrimination in a passage in which the Duke taxes his *Last Duchess*:

> She had
> A heart—how shall I say?—too soon made glad,
> Too easily impressed; she liked whate'er
> She looked on, and her looks went everywhere,
> Sir, 'twas all one! . . .
> Who'd stoop to blame
> This sort of trifling? . . .
> . . . and say, "Just this
> Or that in you disgusts me; here you miss
> Or there exceed the mark."

Browning goes beyond discrimination to flag a triple instance of discretion, the Duchess's want of it, the Duke's self-satisfied restraint in not pointing it out to her while disclosing it to the emissary.

Discretion in this sense is the social corollary of discrimination. Earlier we discussed discretion as essential to civility.[125] Discretion more generally is the exercise by the statesman, judge, politician, policeman, or spouse of whether to apply a rule in the light of factors *not* expressed in the rule itself. Its exercise implies

---

125. The depreciation of discretion and the decline of civility are startlingly evident in the promotion of "in your face" codes of conduct, management styles, and perhaps, playfully, patterns of ties.

a recognition that the rule or usual course of conduct should be modified because of such external factors. Logically, the appeal to factors not expressed in the rule itself is by appeal to a higher criterion such as fairness or appropriateness. But this appeal is implicit, subconscious, and usually defies articulation. Discretion is an exercise of judgment that presupposes discrimination.

Behind talk of discrimination is the idea of quality. We feel that those we respect have an eye for quality where it counts. Talk of quality broadens to talk of style or class, as in "a classy dress," "a classy mountain," "a class act." But the feel for quality requires to be coupled with a second-order feel for the appropriateness of its *degree* to the matter at hand in the sense of the first-cited passage from Aristotle. Sometimes these qualities are in point. At other times, our judgment that considerations of quality or style are inappropriate feeds back (possibly as a protective mechanism) to suppress or even shut down our sensibilities.

Considerations of discrimination and discretion prompt us to amplify our first-order faculties of intelligence and imagination. What needs to be added is *perception*. It is said that perception is theory laden. But for all that, at the relevant explanatory level the capacity for acuity is best understood in a veridical sense. Neither do we need apologies to use an ocular metaphor for understanding. Perception, as it functions as a precondition of discrimination, travels with both intelligence and imagination—a keen mind's eye. But for it to see, an attitudinal corollary to objectivity is required: a wide-eyed appreciation that there are things out there to be observed and differences to be distinguished.[126]

These first-order faculties, then, and judgment that passes on them are at hand to deal with what is around us. The ambiguity of the world calls for choice. The neutral indeterminate events that confront us require us, perhaps other creatures, to make decisions

---

126. Davidson has emphasized the dominant part played by intersubjectivity in the intertwined development of language and thought. On a down-to-earth level, we witness an ongoing role for intersubjectivity in stretching our imagination to see ourselves as others do, monitoring their and our perceptions, passing judgment and modifying ourselves in modest ways accordingly.

nonstop. We are decision machines. Witness the use of "should," "ought," "may," and "will." Most are unreflective and blur into habit, but many constitute judgments. These are made in the context of our purposes, goals, and ideals. But because of the mismatching of the world with ideals, compromise is inevitable. What degree of imperfection, of nonsatisfaction, are we prepared to accept? The parallel consideration is the inevitability of risk. What degree of risk are we ready to take? If Evolution is seen as Grand Tinker patching and fixing what's broke, then we can think of our puny selves stickhandling our way through the maze of events. How we cope forms our lives and us.

As judgment is linked to character so character, in the sense of personality, is linked to morality. Of moral qualities, courage is perhaps paramount, for behind honesty is the courage to be so. And honesty in turn is tied to the Spinozan dispassionate, objective cast of mind. Here we should note that the fallout from the shift of responsibility from the private to the public domain is the inevitable decline in the quality of moral judgments—not because of any lack of goodwill, but because of the coarse grain of institutional decisions. Moral issues such as tolerance, fair treatment, and generosity depend on delicate modulation of inner rules not available to the blunt weapons of the law, no matter how lightly wielded. Yet it is moot whether the inadequacies of marshalling our individual moral mechanism in curing specific ills call for intervention by the state.

The presupposition of an ideal dispassionate, objective cast of mind is denied by deconstructionists. It has been pointed out by David Lehman that stripping away biases in a text of any number of *isms* cannot lead to the deconstruction of concepts without an ultimate contradiction:

> The characteristic assumptions of deconstruction—its profoundly antihumanist drift—have a nightmarish side. What happens if you deconstruct history? What happens if you accept the deconstructive dogma that, as Paul de Man puts it, "the bases for historical knowledge are not empirical facts but written texts, even if these texts masquerade in the guise of wars or revolutions"? What happens when you deconstruct the

subject, the self, the human protagonist? Tzvetan Todorov, a commanding figure among French structuralists, has grave doubts about the poststructuralist agenda. In an arresting phrase, Todorov writes that "it is not possible, without inconsistency, to defend human rights with one hand and deconstruct the idea of humanity with the other."

(1991, 81)

Radical deconstruction is too easy an out. After all, doubting everything has been old hat since Descartes. There is a hidden premise in the deconstructionist view of an epistemic split between concepts and humdrum facts. Yet if such a split cannot be justified, one is dragged back to a realist position that embraces both. It is precisely because there is always some validity to deconstructive techniques,[127] and because the resulting options laid before us are so rich that the challenge to judgment becomes acute. When we confront the pieces spread out we are sometimes brought up short by the palpable reality of this concept rather than that.[128]

---

127. Deconstruction as fun is another matter. A favorite is Richard Rand's comparison of Jacques Derrida to the convicted junk bond king Michael Milken, on which Lehman comments (1991, 37):

Rand's letter reads like an unconscious self-parody, but a brilliant one—you have to pinch yourself to remember that his intent is to *praise* Derrida by linking his methods to those of Wall Street's disgraced prince of leverage. . . . And perhaps there *is* something in Rand's analogy. Junk bonds, the apotheosis of an age of greed, are high-risk, high-yield debt securities used to finance corporate takeovers. Isn't it possible that Derrida and his cronies have aimed at doing something comparable in the academic marketplace, palming off a debased currency of empty "signifiers" for which they nevertheless claim value and prestige.

128. Zeno's paradoxes (Achilles, the arrow) come to mind in this running away from reality to a construct that may be inappropriate or incompatible with the central concept in issue. The way through the paradoxes is to start out with the reality of *motion* and its defining constituents (distance and *periods* of time) and to see *instant* of time (the concept that is the root of the paradoxes) is a figment without reality, inconsistent with motion, although useful in solving other puzzles.

Judgment's job is to weigh the alternatives and build from there. This synthetic process implies the exercise of judgment in which we aim to act judicially, that is, dispassionately and disinterestedly. We may fail, but that is not at issue. What is, is that there are instances where we agree that agents do so act. In order to reinforce the centrality of judgment I have stressed the indeterminacy in the minutiae of our experiences. It might be said I have deconstructed them. But acknowledging this indeterminacy is the first and essential step to reconstructing durable concepts. So we sometimes feel that rules, principles, and generalizations are paramount. At other times that there are only single events and chaotic contingencies. The dilemma is that neither necessarily holds. What runs through our daily decisions are judgments on how seriously to take such rules, principles, and generalizations on which we depend, knowing that they are open at any moment to defeat by the infinity of variables. Here we need have recourse to our inchoate ideals. It is hard to shake the conviction that our character is tied to this reservoir, for these ideals are indeed us. Hence the throw-away line: "She can't be all bad if she believes such and such."

Credibility

We live in a credit society. Our banking system operates on credit, not only in the sense of debt, but in the sense of credibility. You can cash a check at the bank because your bank is prepared to accept it at face value. The bank has a degree of faith in its customers. Language and therefore communication also depends on credibility.[129] We must assume that others mean more or less what they say. In a wider sense credibility is at the heart of human relationships including those having cognitive impact. Similarly, if we don't have faith in the credibility of others because of the display of certain personality traits, we may lose confidence in their judgment. Of course specialist judgments may sometimes over-

---

129. See the discussion of the principle of charity by Davidson (1984, 27) in which he draws on Quine's ideas in *Word and Object.*

ride character deficiencies. A president from whom we would not buy a used car may still display sound judgment on foreign policy. But doubts linger. We have seen that legal systems through the requirement for evidence, hence witnesses, depend directly on credibility. The stark exercise of judgment required of the judge or jury is whether to believe one witness rather than another and to what extent. Credibility is a precondition to the weighting of the evidence.

The principle of charity attributes prima facie credibility to statements. It assumes good faith in the sense of no deliberate attempt to mislead. In order for words to work in communication, we must take people at theirs. But in the interesting cases we proceed beyond that initial impression, for we are all unwitting promoters of our beliefs. In order to determine credibility, judgment is required not only of the speaker's judgmental faculties but of his objectivity. On this point, when the personality appears unduly involved in the telling, watch out. Credibility also applies to art through the ingredient of sincerity. Stanley Cavell (1969) suggests that we treat art objects as we do people; that is, we test them for their sincerity. There is a carry-over of the integrity we attribute to persons to works of art that they produce, and vice versa.

There remains the nag of the effect of seemingly trivial matters on our view of the integrity of the personality and thus credibility generally. Does a person's outlandish dress, hairstyle, or personal habits say something to us about his judgment on other matters? There is an inward uneasiness that it should not, which causes the bother. Sometimes doubts about the other's judgment can be rationalized by identifying an inner need to display, which may be inconsistent with the dispassionate state of mind, that is, the submerging of the personal, required for judgment. Sometimes the doubt can be rationalized by identifying an insensitivity to the opinion or feelings of others which may be relevant to take into account in forming a judgment.

The connection between credibility and appearance suggests a more comprehensive conclusion. We are reminded of W. H. Auden's musing quoted earlier: "Does God ever judge us by appearances? I suspect He does. . . ." This recalls Lincoln's purported remark that after the age of forty we are all responsible for our faces. Ultimately, we must take appearance in its totality. But we have to read it right. Just as we judge people by their judgments (the more serious the subject, as in the choice of a political running mate, the more severe our judgment of theirs), so inversely we assess the confidence we place in judgments by the character of their maker.

But the judgment of character itself untainted by stereotypical attitudes, perhaps the counsel of perfection, is not always appropriate. Goethe, in a passage in the *Italian Journey* reminiscent of the first cited passage of Aristotle, reflects on the scales appropriate to the psychology of friendship:

> I am beginning to get along better with other people. The important thing to remember is always to weigh them by the shopkeeper's scales and never by the goldsmith's, as friends, in hypochondriac or exacting moods, are only too apt to do with each other, alas.

Development

The ancients have provided us with two contrasting figures of judgmental qualities defining the personality. Odysseus is realized as a character not so much by his vaunted cunning or courage but by his steady, rounded judgment so that the rare exceptions prompted by curiosity or pride, such as his taunting of the cyclops, give dramatic force. Against this buoyant prototype is the sober Roman *gravitas* of the elder Brutus who calmly condemned his sons to death as traitors. But for us an impression of someone's judgment is in the main built up from common sense displayed in dozens of humdrum decisions. There is an element of tautology here because common sense is simply the working of good judgment in a minor key. But the tautology is not trivial for it indicates the inseparable relationship between judgment and the face we display to the world. The first signs of common sense in an infant are heartwarming because of their confirmation of humanity.

From then on, will judgment develop more or less on its own like language or will a certain environment be necessary to its development? To the extent the ability to exercise judgment is not inborn, it would seem to follow that upbringing and education must play a part in its development. Knowledge does not guarantee good judgment. Nevertheless, a wide command of the facts may result in an informed judgment in a greater variety of situations. Here "facts" include facts about ideas. It is therefore tempting to speculate that a wide humanist education rather than a narrow professional one may tend to develop judgment over a wider range. Such a broad education anchored in the humanities, together with a notion of the fundamentals of the natural and social sciences, leads to the classic ideal of *Bildung*.

Take the example of history. The sight of the young confronting ideas brings home how three-dimensional ideas are. Not merely ideas about ideas, but ideas about events. Apart from the understanding of the surface concept, there is the horizontal reach to related ideas of which they may have some grasp. But without consciousness of what ideas have gone through at the hands of history, they remain husks.[130] Yet again how much weight is to be placed on that extra dimension? Can a politician, an economist, or indeed anyone who purports to affect society be credible without history? Can anybody under thirty be trusted? But *which* history, one might ask. Not necessarily that to which one is genetically connected, for ideas can migrate in a flash and settle in unlikely places. Witness the shift from tundra to quadrangle, from *apparatchik* to capitalist.

To read well and deeply must mean a discarding and a bringing together. On the other hand, postmodernists such as Michel Foucault, Jacques Derrida, and other Continental philosophers[131]

---

130. "Gone through" is at the back of much aesthetic sensibility: the patina on a dug-up bronze, the plaster walls of a Tuscan village, and the true blue of jeans faded on the range rather than by bleach. Is there here as well as in the world of ideas a common prizing of a complex layering?

131. The common reference to "Continental" and other geographic labels attached to philosophy gives one pause. We may appreciate different styles, schools, and doing things in literature peculiar to places and cul-

overdose on the cultural obstacles to the accessibility of a common viewpoint. Where is the balance to be struck? It is precisely this culture-laden turn of mind encapsulated by *Bildung* that brings in judgment. By expanding the picture it invokes the responsibility to size it up. Paradoxically, by including implicit cultural elements in cognition, which, it is argued, itself requires an objective judgmental function, a shift to *Bildung* stiffens our backbone against the drift to cultural relativism.

The question of the desirability of a certain kind of academic education was raised partially to dismiss it. There are too many counterexamples of persons with little or no academic education who give unmistakable evidence of sound judgment.[132] Street-smarts is simply an extreme form. With them exposure to a humanist education would simply widen the scope of judgment. Is judgment then largely an inborn gift?

> Good sense which only is the gift of Heaven,
> And though no science, fairly worth the seven.
> (Alexander Pope, *Moral Essays*)

But to the extent that judgment is not due solely to an inborn capacity, yet is also not taught directly, it must be acquired from diffuse experience. Its most fruitful source may be the interaction

---

tures. Literature while universal in some respects is in another the expression of the regional differences and the language in which it takes form. Not so science. Whatever its shifting paradigms, it is an oxymoron to think of science at a given time as culture specific. One would have thought the same of philosophy which deals with matters even more universal, fundamental, and comprehensive than science. It says something about the paradoxical place philosophy occupies, perhaps inevitably, on the literature/science spectrum to find this late in the day treatment in terms of French, English, German, and American philosophy. See G. Borradori, *The American Philosopher* (1994), which records conversations with philosophers as diverse as Quine, Putnam, Nozick, Rorty, Kuhn, Stanley Cavell, Arthur Danto, and Alasdair MacIntyre.

132. As E. M. Forster acknowledges in *The Longest Journey*: "Mr. Ansell was not merely a man of some education; he had what no education can bring—the power of detecting what is important." I owe the reference to this rare tribute to importance to Mary Swann.

with role models where judgment can be observed. Here the perceptive person will absorb the tacit lessons of how judgments are made. This raises the well-known connection between judgment and examples. While Kant had strong views on the impossibility of teaching judgment, he did give weight to the beneficial effect of examples. He continues his earlier cited observations on professionals:

> Or the error may be due to his not having received, through examples and actual practice, adequate training for this particular act of judgment. Such sharpening of the judgment is indeed the one great benefit of examples. . . . Examples are thus the go-cart of judgment; and those who are lacking in the natural talent can never dispense with them.
>
> (Kant 1985, 178)

But Kant is perhaps too sanguine. Examples may themselves be no more than examples of judgment rather than means of achieving it. There is a temptation to think of examples as playing the same role in judgment as particular observations do in inductive inference. But induction, whatever its deeper problematic, assumes relevant similarities. Judgment on the other hand is brought into play just because there is no obvious similar case to follow.[133] The most that can be learned from examples is not the reaching of the same conclusion but broad procedural clues on ways of arrival.[134]

---

133. In a deeper sense, one can ask what legitimizes the use of examples at all, or of seeing something as similar to or as an example of something else. Presumably some highly attenuated judgment of appropriateness is involved. Irene Harvey puts the question to Derrida: "In short, is it not a metaphysical gesture par excellence to transform the 'given particular' (whatever it may be) into an *example* of a non-given generality?" (Sallis 1988, 68).

134. Wittgenstein also sees a nexus between examples and judgment as practice: "We do not learn the practice of making empirical judgments by learning rules: we are taught judgments and their connection with other judgments" (1969, 140). Again, "My judgments themselves characterize the way I judge, characterize the nature of judgment" (1969, 149).

The fact that we feel comfortable in attributing good judgment to others without further ado serves as a clue to answer how such judgment is acquired. Is it inborn, sure to expose itself over time, or can it be taught? Can fitting and weighting be taught? Can a feel for importance and appropriateness be acquired? Can it be transferred from one field to another? While the subject awaits empirical study, the phenomenon of good judgment exercised in alien fields implies that it is not experience in that particular field which is essential. So it would appear that if such judgment is not inborn but acquired through environmental factors, it must at some deep level be learning to recognize the elements of judgment: to recognize importance and appropriateness *generally* and to manipulate them.

We talk of the cultivation of a critical faculty in say, fifteenth-century Italian painting or in a particular field of legal practice. We seem to believe that with limits such efforts can meet with success. But we rarely hear of attempts to cultivate our generic judgmental faculties. The reason is that in a specific field we pick up which features to attend to, those that are important and appropriate. Hence within limits, in a given field, judgment can be learned, although progress may be glacially slow. Even here guides may fail us when we come to the interesting novel cases. It is from these various considerations that it is appropriate to hazard a hypothesis that there is a generic faculty of judgment.

Such a generic faculty is displayed by the art of conversation which, as Michael Oakeshott has pointed out, is a distinguishing essential mark of our civilization. We saw earlier that a structural turn of mind appears to be critical to judgment. Whether it can be taught by admonitions or otherwise is at best moot. Some believe that it can be absorbed through the pores.[135] Some believe that

---

135. Oakeshott quotes from the reflections of an Eton master, William Cory, who understood education as a preparation for participation in conversation (Oakeshott 1962, 200):

[Y]ou go to a great school not so much for knowledge as for arts and habits; for the habit of attention, for the art of expression, for the art of assuming at a moment's notice a new intellectual posi-

progress can be made through immersion in studies rich in theory, where a certain sort of structure is close to the surface: logic, grammar, philosophy, and law. It is significant that we speak not of teaching judgment but of developing it. But even here, beyond a certain age the prospect seems bleak. The analogy that comes to mind is a natural aptitude for sports. Training will only take you so far. With judgment it would appear to be far less so. In the face of the manifest role of judgment, if it *were* possible to develop it, why would nobody do it? With respect to intelligence, coaching for IQ and SAT tests is common. No comparable help is available for judgment. While much requires empirical investigation, the apathy toward improvement of judgment implies recognition that not much can be done.

On reflection, it is not surprising that little attention has been paid to judgment in the academy. It is not so much that there is occasional truth to the picture of the absent-minded professor. It is rather that the role of comprehension and creativity, rather than judgment, is at a premium in the academic world. While judgment is essential to cognition, its role is not apparent at a functional level in the classroom or the cloistered study in the same way it is everywhere apparent in the world outside.

The indispensability of background knowledge and context has cropped up at various places in the discussion. It is of course essential to the grasp of meanings. It turned up in the technical analysis of what constitutes evidence. Psychologists tell us how

---

tion, for the art of entering quickly into another person's thoughts, for the habit of submitting to censure and refutation, for the art of indicating assent or dissent in graduated terms, for the habit of regarding minute points of accuracy, for the art of working out what is possible in a given time, for taste, discrimination, for mental courage and mental soberness.

In a negative sense the quaintness of this passage, which implies a judgmental turn of mind, suggests that if judgment cannot be learned it may at least be dulled or hindered from natural development by the obverse quality of stridency. We might go on to ask what sort of society is hospitable to the development and wide diffusion of Cory's qualities of mind.

the framing of questions determines preferences. It haunts attempts of AI researchers to formalize thought processes where they surface in the concept of the frame. The trouble is that the very impetus to the importation of frames (to circumscribe the context) makes the determination of the frame an infinite regress. What is the frame of context that defines the frame itself? Background knowledge is also brought in by the debate about the *ceteris paribus* (i.e., all other things being equal) qualification to scientific laws.[136] For it takes judgment to see if all other things (all relevant things) are equal. Generally, we saw that past knowledge (a background of beliefs) is essential to the acquisition of new knowledge. Now we see its presence in the shift from knowledge to *Bildung*. Yet the access to and application of background knowledge is itself dependent upon judgments: in selecting the relevant bits from the undifferentiated mass and in attributing appropriate weights.

The themes sounded here of the primacy of background (horizon) and the objectivity of importance (significance) are tied to self-definition by Charles Taylor:

> It may be important that my life be chosen, as John Stuart Mill asserts in *On Liberty*, but unless some options are more significant than others, the very idea of self-choice falls into triviality and hence incoherence. Self-choice as an ideal makes sense only because some *issues* are more significant than others. I couldn't claim to be a self-chooser, and deploy a whole Nietzschean vocabulary of self-making, just because I choose steak and fries over poutine for lunch. Which issues are significant, *I* do not determine. If I did, no issue would be significant. But then the very ideal of self-choosing as a *moral ideal* would be impossible.
>
> So the ideal of self-choice supposes that there are *other* issues of significance beyond self-choice. The ideal couldn't stand alone, because it requires a horizon of issues of importance, which help define the *respects* in which self-making is significant.
>
> (1991, 39)

---

136. See the discussion of the issue particularly with respect to psychology between Stephen Schiffer and Jerry Fodor, "Ceteris Paribus Laws," *Mind* 100, no. 1 (January 1991).

Rationality

Readers may have asked themselves how this judgmental function with its intimate connection to cognition jibes with what has in recent philosophy been treated as rationality. In the distinctions drawn earlier I have attempted a partial answer. S. L. Hurley's *Natural Reasons* provides the opportunity to address the subject more comprehensively. A brief discussion of her views on the rationality of moral decisions will throw my own position into relief.

For much of the way Hurley and I travel on parallel roads that traverse mental events, decision theory, jurisprudence, social choice, politics, and personality. Hers is the higher road, higher because it proceeds in the traditional philosophical way through the concepts of preferences and reasons to ethical values. Mine passes through the psychological and methodological phenomena of day-to-day decisions across an even wider stretch of experience, touched only peripherally by the higher road. Hers leads to the objectivity of values while in a sense my road starts from there. I ask: what happens when you confront the decision with a full quiver of values. Thus what is said here can be seen as a companion piece to hers. It tops up her treatment of *deliberation* by pointing out one sort, the exercise of judgment, blows it up, and distinguishes it from other sorts. What I see as the key psychological and methodological stopping points of importance and appropriateness are off her route.

So while my views can be seen as an appendix to Hurley, they must in an opposite sense be seen as the invisible foundation on which her edifice depends. For it is my argument that recognitions of importance and appropriateness, and thus relevance and weight, underlie not only practical and moral reasoning but the whole cognitive structure. The issue comes to a head in applying rules, values, and concepts to the particular case. Here Hurley moves back and forth from values in general to particular moral decisions without sometimes catching the significance of the move. She speaks of "ethical beliefs" and "conflicting reasons and values." Surely, on an abstract level this is a dying issue. Consistency and coherence at this lofty level does not seem an expensive enterprise. The conceptual price tags come into view only in the unfolding multiplicity of applications.

Such a determination of abstract values is by definition *a priori* any particular application. On the other hand, as Hurley admits, any theory to justify reasons (make them cohere) for any particular act can only be arrived at *a posteriori,* after the judgment (a theme I developed under "Courts"). But after the fact, one can rationalize much in the name of coherence. To what rule (concept) do we appeal to determine coherence? She gives two examples, one of deciding on which of three persons to bestow a precious violin. The other, which of three critically ill persons to treat first. The analysis is well conceived in terms of what the deliberator may take into account in making the choice but, not surprisingly, the denouement is left to "salient enough features of human nature," "hypotheses about the relative weight of the principles in various circumstances," and "weighted and qualified principles." If I understand her aright, Hurley would here press coherence in some unspecified way to resolve the salience, weight, and priority issues. But to do so is to breach the Kantian injunction that ultimately we can't (and I believe don't) appeal to a rule to apply a rule.

Now how does this relate judgment to rationality? Rationality holds out two promises. One is that what it reaches purports to be true. To that extent judgment is consistent with rationality. The second promise is that the process to reach its destination is in theory transparent; that is, the process can be made conscious, laid out, dissected, and itself judged. That is a promise that judgment cannot keep—except in the limited way discussed earlier. The reasonableness of giving reasons for a decision is the entrée to the objective world. But rationality, if it is to mean more than good thinking, demands a procedure be put up to decide among them. Ultimately, we cannot even in theory prescribe how an agreed basket of values, "reasons" (I would rather suggest "considerations"), will be applied in a specified case. Out goes consistency, a hallmark of rationality. Earlier I said considerations were the generic feedstock of judgments. Considerations live in the air, as against reasons that live to ground conclusions. We *raise* considerations but later *give* reasons, which may include more than considerations.[137] Talk of reasons ends up as Gilbert Harman (1977) does, in talk of "stronger" reasons. Absent logical deduction, this reduces to appeal in some opaque way to importance and appropriateness. One can always give reasons. The point is that in questions of judgment we can never tell in advance which reasons will prevail. The varied examples given in the preceding pages serve to show that no rule seems able to determine how these considerations will play out in individual decisions. To subsume this discontinuous process under a broader rationality is to leach out the term's explanatory power.[138] So,

---

137. See footnote 140 on the ambiguity of "reasons." Consider the example from Wall Street of the relative value to be given to brand name franchises as against private labels. The considerations have always been in the air; it is the attributable weight that swings wildly.

138. On the heels of Hurley is Robert Nozick's *The Nature of Rationality* (1993), in which he extends rationality until it ends simply in good thinking. Following his extension of rationality to imagination, Marcia Cavell (1993, 138) ascribes rationality to emotions as well. She rightly points out that thought is a necessary condition of emotions (at least some) and indeed that infants could not feel shame or pride without learning the appropriate thoughts. There is then a jump "that thought is a necessary condition for emotion, not its accomplice but part of its very constitution; that emotions are therefore neither beyond the reach nor beneath reason but, like beliefs, the sort of thing which can be said to be both rational and irrational." But rationality is not having thoughts but what we do with them. It is a justificatory process. As I understand her, Cavell believes that the rational justification for an emotion is to identify a belief not simply as the cause of the emotion but as part of it. What would an irrational emotion be? In the course of discussing Freud's account of his patient the Rat Man, she continues (p. 141) that emotions are attitudes toward propositions which she calls emotional Intentionality. But while it is perceptive to realize that in some sense emotions can be said to reach out and be "about objects," as pointed out in footnote 26, the aboutness is a specious intentionality encouraged by an indiscriminate use of "propositional attitudes." Isn't it clearer to keep beliefs and emotions logically distinct so we can make sense of statements such as "The belief excited her but left her friend cold" without attributing a second belief to the excitement?

with respect to particular judgments, the third cheer for rationality must be withheld, perhaps forever.

But the fact that we cannot logically track and predict a judgment does not mean that such judgments are not in the main objective. I spoke earlier of reaching Davidson's position of "a shared view of how things are" through the back door. I can do so only tenuously by arguing backward from the now familiar beliefs in (a) a general principle of coherence, (b) the interaction of fact and value, (c) our knowledge being of the only world there is, to which beliefs is now contributed the argument made here that (d) determinations of importance and appropriateness are an essential ingredient of that knowledge.

This belief in the opaque objectivity of judgments in turn entails the belief in the necessity of a line somewhere between preferences and values. To arrive at her destination of demonstrating the objectivity of ethical choices, Hurley makes much of the fact that our individual preferences are themselves grounded in shared values. Of course common values, just like the rest of our makeup and environment, enter into our preferences. But the significant point is that the function of *preference* in the language is just to make room for cases that don't. When we talk of preference we emphasize a person's *own* relative desires regardless of values, notwithstanding how those desires are formed. Conflating preference with value cuts against the case for the objectivity of the latter. We need to face up to the existence of such an undefinable crooked line between value and (mere) preference. Significantly, a clue to the line is sometimes seen in the appropriateness of a reference to judgment. We prefer democratic society because we judge it to be best. We prefer thick-cut marmalade, period.[139] The adoption of an undiagnosed preference/probability formula, even as modified by Hurley, will not serve to justify the rationality of individual choices.

This discontinuity between preference and value coexists with

---

139. But if this seems plain, the application of this test to the elemental constituents of art, say, the colors, the sounds, raises a question for aesthetics. If it is this very shade of blue introduced by the artist which draws us, can we say we prefer it because we judge it best?

the other discontinuities that we have observed between: rules and their application, prediction and indeterminacy, thinking and neurophysical events, and thought and its subject. So while notwithstanding these gaps we can reach a faith (reasoned in the backward way sketched out above) in an overarching monism, we must recognize that it is anomalous in more than one way.

Weigh(t)ing Again

At the beginning of *Philosophical Explanations* Robert Nozick (1981) paints the picture of a comprehensive philosophical theory as a Greek temple, rather than a tower that totters when its foundation is undermined. The bombardment of criticism can destroy the coherence of a temple but a few columns may be left standing to weather. A column that should survive is his emphasis (in contrast to Hurley) on the phenomenon of choice and *weigh(t)ing*:

> Making some choices feels like this. There are various reasons for and against doing each of the alternative actions or courses of actions one is considering, and it seems and feels as if one could do any one of them. In considering the reasons, mulling them over, one arrives at a view of which reasons are more important, which ones have more weight. One decides which reasons to act on; or one may decide to act on none of them but to seek instead a new alternative since none previously considered was satisfactory.
>
> After the choice, however, others will say we were caused to act by the considerations[140] which were (or turned out to be)

---

140. "Caused to act by the considerations" calls for comment. Nozick appears to follow Davidson's position that the reason for an action is its cause. The theory is attractive on several counts. It seems to sharpen the notion that a certain reason rather than another is responsible for an act. It also lends a semantic plausibility to the view that our conduct is rational. But there are misgivings reinforced by Nozick's reference to "considerations." As discussed above, it is now accepted by those who follow Davidson that there are two distinct languages that describe the mind; one the language of physics, the other of psychology. The force of the theory is

more weighty. And it is not just others. We too, in looking back at our past actions, will see which reasons swayed us and will view (accepting) those considerations as having caused us to act as we did. Had we done the other act, though, acting on the opposing considerations, we (along with the others) would have described those considerations as causing us to do that other act. Whichever act we do, the (different) background considerations exist which can be raised to causal status. Which considerations will be so raised depends upon which act we do. Does the act merely show which of the considerations was the weightier cause, or does the decision make one of them weightier?

The reasons do not come with previously given precisely specified weights; the decision process is not one of discovering such precise weights but of assigning them. The process not only weighs reasons it (also) weights. At least, so it sometimes feels. This process of weighting may focus narrowly, or involve considering or deciding what sort of person one wishes to be, what sort of life one wishes to lead.

What picture of choice emerges if we take seriously the feeling that the (precise) weights to be assigned to reasons is

---

that while it is clear that in some unknown way physical events are responsible for the mental events described by psychology, it is systematically impossible to relate a specific physical event to a specific mental event. But what needs adding is that there is a third language that describes the life of the mind, that which refers to ideas *qua* ideas. The gulf between the language of psychology and that of ideas is that between thinking and thought. Now, the ambiguous term *reasons* has a foot in both camps. On the one hand it can refer to a mental event (motives, emotions) in which case it qualifies as a cause of another mental event. On the other hand it can mean an idea, including the one at the end of a thought process. But ideas are not events, although they need admission to our ontology. Taken as ideas they have no causal efficacy; and *considerations* are ideas (ones we take into account). But now comes the white knight of *belief* to leap the gulf. For, being mental events, occurrent beliefs are not logically precluded from causing others. In some mysterious way a belief *accepts* the thought or idea and makes it its own. It is the accepting that is the event. But the gulf is merely papered over. We no more know—can do no more than state—how ideas become the content of belief events (that may cause other *distinguishable* (Thalberg 1972, 50) events, than we can explain such particular mental events by physical events. Nozick is talking loosely.

"up to us"? It is causally undetermined (by prior factors) which
of the acts we will decide to do. It may be causally determined
that certain reasons are reasons (in the one direction or the
other) but there is no prior causal determination of the precise
weight each reason will have in competition with others.

(Nozick 1981, 294)

Here we have a compressed account of what constitutes the
event or series of events we call the exercise of judgment that we
have been looking at from various angles. In normal discourse
when we say "weigh" we assume that the things weighed have
the weights which we are determining. On the other hand, when
we *weight* we understand that we attach or attribute a weight *to*
something. The clear distinction between the two is, as Nozick
suggests, blurred and indeed may disappear in our actual judgments. Again we see a similar fault line running, as we did
between preference and value, crisscrossed a dozen times when
we seek to understand and justify our choices.

Nozick is concerned with choice in the rarified atmosphere of
free will as a foundation of ethics. What I have felt compelled to
show, skimming over diverse areas of experience, is that judgment is as central to the humdrum substratum of our lives as it is
to the twin peaks in the sights of philosophers—knowledge of
reality and free will to do the right thing. The issue of indeterminacy that dogs moral decisions stalks all judgments.

Although we must give research a chance, indeed a challenge
to uncover the psychological roots of this weigh(t)ing process—
in short how judgments are made—we must be skeptical about
the distance it will travel before striking a Heisenbergian wall.
We saw earlier that decision theory has so far succeeded only in
pushing back judgment to concepts of weight, similarity, and
context. Furthermore, research seeks generalizations that range
over classes of events. How then is generalization on this subject
possible where every event shapes its own judgment in its own
way, except in the very broad, rough way attempted here?

The wonder is that for all the indeterminacy in judgment,
there are so few lapses at the common-sense end of the scale.
Thus our shared world. But we pay the price at the other extreme.

Rarely in disagreement on values as such, but in the agony of their application, in the degree of trust we must place on our ultimate judgments, we float abandoned without markers except for the faint lights that blink inside. If *King Lear* is the tragedy that unfolds from one monumental misjudgment, cannot *Hamlet* be seen as the tragedy that we have no appeal to a higher certainty, that our judgments will remain forever ours?

Getting It Right

This essay is perforce not only about the elements of judgment but about what judgment aims at, getting things right. For "right" is judgment's lifelong partner just as truth is paired with knowledge. *Getting things right* also enters into a consideration of several obstacles to a unified field theory of judgment. We have seen that in the paradigm cases of exercising judgment considerations of importance and appropriateness lie just below the surface. In the plain vanilla case of deciding the right thing to do, these considerations have intuitive validity. But how do they relate to Kant's conception of judgment as the application of a rule to a specific instance, or to Frege's concept of judgment as recognizing the truth of a thought? To take Frege first, recognizing the truth of a thought or proposition is, after all, simply one kind, perhaps the most important kind of decision. There is nothing in Frege's concept which precludes the place of importance and appropriateness in determining what that decision should be in a particular instance. Frege's view of judgment as truth recognition (keeping in mind his chief concern for logical truth) can be extended, although in a tortured way, to embrace the exercise of judgment generally. For we can recast "I judge A the right action to take" as "I recognize that the sentence *A is the right action to take* is true." On this level a strained reconciliation with Frege is possible.

Kant's concept of rule application is more problematic. Hume, Kant, and Wittgenstein each in a different way imply that judgment is shrouded in mystery, an epistemological dead end. So in Kant's sense it will to a large extent remain. Yet insight is gained in recalling what is at work in the application by courts of legal rules. To see that a law applies is to recognize the salient features of the case at hand and to match them with the salient features of the legal rule. There is an open texture to the rule and the case, requiring determinations of appropriateness in reading both. Fitting and weighting will determine the choice. So perhaps in a less perceptible way with the application of rules generally, until the process disappears or becomes vestigial, at which point we no longer speak of exercising judgment but simply of applying the rule. But where the process is discernible, while the mystery remains, it is pushed a step back.

We saw that judgments can be tortured into recognitions of truth. But is it not less contrived to accommodate true statements into a more comprehensive category of getting things right? Usage hints at the primacy of the judgmental function in cognition. Instead of the sobriquet of truth, we often talk broadly of "getting it right." We saw that this attribution is the acknowledgment of the success of a judgmental function—the right attribution of weights, importance, and appropriateness, the right pitch; in sum, tailoring the verbal formula to the circumstances. This last consideration expands judgment from a critical faculty into a creative, synthetic one. What is out there is ambivalent and ambiguous and it is the judgmental function that copes with this ambivalence. Judgment in this sense thus goes beyond recognizing the truth of a thought (belief) in Frege's sense, to *forming* the true thought—taking the clay of ideas and modeling it into what is right there and then. Judgment thus has a role in concept formation, in determining the degree to which subsidiary concepts should find a place in the end idea. Standing back to check whether the new-made thought is right can itself be thought of as invoking the same process one step removed. It will be said that so expanding the province of judgment invades the territory of intelligence and imagination. So it does. But while there are no boundaries in the mind,[141] and the three faculties run into each

---

141. We are reminded of Davidson (1980, 231) "emphasizing the holistic character of the cognitive field" and the necessity to "impose conditions of coherence, rationality and consistency" in forming the picture of

other at the borders, distinctions are salvaged by acknowledging that reference does not coincide, that each can be present without much of the others.

Note that the stable state for *truth* is as a noun as well as an adjective[142] where it applies to sentences and statements. *Right,* on the other hand, is only at home as an adjective or adverb. The grammatical ambivalence of "right" in "getting it right" reflects much of what has been said about the multiple aspects of judgment. Does it act as an adjective by modifying the conclusion ("it") or as an adverb by modifying the process ("getting")? In any event, right has a broader reach than truth by applying to thoughts, decisions, and actions. While truth remains a backstop, getting it right is the more comprehensive and user-friendly concept. One can get something "pretty right" but not "pretty true," "just right" but not "just true." And it is significant that when we get something absolutely (just) right we tend to call it true. Truth is bivalent, right isn't. But both are "evidence transcendent," to use Crispin Wright's (1993) term. Truth as a language-centered attribute, a stand-alone concept, floats free of pragmatic origins while right harkens to the generic judgmental process and thus straddles the entire cognitive function.

Admittedly, with respect to truth it is salutary to stick to a narrow conception: Tarski's (1949) elegant Convention T (the sentence "snow is white" is true if, and only if, snow is white). But the tighter the focus of what is so illumined, the larger the area left in the dark.[143] How can we escape coming to grips with the seeming semantic satisfaction that lies outside the blessed circle?

---

the mind. While I understand he holds that rationality includes the judgmental function, such tacit inclusion under that heading, I would argue, obscures the critical distinctions.

142. See J. L. Austin's emphasis on the adjectival: "*In vino,* possibly '*veritas,*' but in a sober symposium, '*verum*' " (Pitcher 1964, 18). One could add, *a fortiori* "rightness" only in the buzz of academic discourse.

143. That is not to say that one can explicate truth beyond Tarski's spare formulation. It would appear that all such "substantial" explications turn out not only circular but empty. Take Crispin Wright's "superassertibility" or Hilary Putnam's souped-up warrant "in ideal epistemic circum-

Metaphors are a good mid-range example of what lies out-side. In one sense "(no) man is an island" is clearly false. But in another sense we have a rough idea of what Donne was getting at, what he meant. He didn't mean just a bit of land surrounded by water. We can expand what we think he meant in a labored way in a few sentences, paragraphs, or a book. But the poetic impact achieved through the juxtaposition of the falseness of the conventional meaning (a defining characteristic of metaphor) and the appropriateness of the secondary meaning will then be lost. Nonetheless, even though this overlapping area is impossible to circumscribe, it has cognitive content. On the other hand, this distinguishing feature of a metaphor's juxtaposition of one nec-essarily false meaning with the truth of another freshly struck, is absent in other poetic devices where the sharp edges of contrast-ed meanings have been ground down or never were. Cleanth Brooks (1947, 200) gives a vivid example of one such device in his discussion of Yvor Winters's account of Browning's use of *wore*: "So wore night; the East was gray." Brooks is right in dis-abusing Winters of the belief in a "literal" meaning together with a second poetic meaning of the word. "Wore" simply means wore, with all its freighted coloring. While Browning's use is right poetically, there can be no other sense in which it is patent-ly false as is the case with metaphor. What we take the metaphor to mean evinces a larger semantic intent which brings into play consideration that its expression is right. Nor is there always a line between metaphorical and "ordinary" usage. It isn't only prose we have unsuspectingly been talking all along but occa-sionally poetry.[144]

---

stances." Isn't the point of "warrant" and "assert" to translate an abstract concept into something do-able ruled out by "ideal"? And ideal epistemic circumstances are only understandable in terms of what is true, and not the other way around.

144. I am indebted to Davidson's provocative, but I believe mistaken, view of metaphors (see "What Metaphors Mean" [1984, 245], and cita-tions of authors discussed). Davidson believes: "A metaphor doesn't say anything beyond its literal meaning (nor does its maker say anything, in using the metaphor, beyond the literal)." He would thus disagree with what

Once it is recognized in the case of metaphor that what lies outside Convention T has cognitive content (that is, the metaphor can be right or wrong),[145] it cannot be written off in Davidson's way as emotional coloring or things simply pointed to. The implication of attributing meaning to the metaphor in the nonliteral sense is to lower our expectations of the definitiveness attainable. If something must give, perhaps it is our concept of having meaning and meaning itself. Perhaps it needs deflation to a rough and ready marker that sometimes does no more than indicate the presence of cognitive content that may be spun out indefinitely. The span of meaning evident in sentences that invite verdicts of right rather than true stretch beyond truth conditions. We are left with the conclusion that in the case of metaphor, and judgment gener-

---

I have been saying. But several of his own examples tell against him. Take "he was burnt up." As Davidson says it now means that "he was very angry." At what point did the metaphor die and the clear second meaning emerge? The answer is at no particular time; two meanings survive. In this case the derived meaning is pretty well given by his paraphrase, but not entirely, the first survives weakly. Then take his treatment of similes. It is just a small jump from similes to metaphors. But Davidson sees no difficulty in saying that similes mean what they say. But isn't the problem identical? If we say "man is like an island," the sentence is clearly false in one way and true, is right (in my sense) in another. He also seems mistaken in comparing the making of a metaphor to telling a lie. "The comparison is apt because lying, like making a metaphor, concerns not the meaning of words but their use." While this makes sense in the case of lying, it does not with metaphor where the use remains descriptive but the description simply complex. Does Davidson really believe that Donne means man is a piece of land surrounded by water, period? Davidson here appears trapped by his pristine concept of meaning tied to Convention T.

145. Here it is easy to allow *representation* to insinuate itself as an entity that is right or wrong. But see Rorty's and John Murphy's summary of their and Davidson's anti-representative views placed under the mantle of a wider pragmatism (Murphy 1990). Perhaps the differences between representationalists and anti-representationalists will settle into a consensus describable paradoxically as platonic pragmatism. That is, beyond all the dogmas, including the split between belief and meaning, lies the acceptance that ideas, no matter how formed historically, have an objectivity, occasional truth, and ontological self-sufficiency not to be gainsaid.

ally, a correspondence relationship is implied that is no less mysterious but no more Platonic than that of language to thought.[146] While it is easy enough to discriminate between differing sorts of judgment, I believe, contrary to Dewey and Rorty, that the aim of getting things right is the principal common feature of all judgment: e.g., a decision to send an angry letter, biting one's tongue (after all, an act of the intellect), a translation of Proust, and a metaphor. There is a temptation to explain these instances psychologically by appealing to a notion of satisfaction. But satisfaction of what? Satisfaction of the peculiarly human need to recognize or formulate a semantic relationship.[147]

So seen, truth is a subclass of getting things right composed of those cases where a Convention T formulation is possible. A bonus of this wider approach is that it leads through the concepts of appropriateness and fit quite naturally into coherence theories and answers some of the charges of antirealists. Alternatively one could say that what is right is always true but at the cost of giving up Convention T, which serves as a refined protocol for single sentences but becomes unwieldy when the matter described requires expansion beyond a single sentence, let alone a book. One way or another we must face up to instances where "rings true" appears manifestly right yet where Convention T is not available. Conversely, why do things jar? Because the sought correspondence has failed. That semantic-type relationships stop at Convention T is simply another dogma.[148]

---

146. See "Thought and Talk" where Davidson (1984, 155) discusses the mutual interdependence of thought and language but stops short of treading on this ground. Also see Burge (1992) on Frege's platonism. I would venture that the reality of thought as prior to language yet requiring expression in it has its epistemic analogue in the reality of the external world as prior to experience yet unknowable without it.

The link between language and thought also goes the other way. Hence the intellectual poverty of multimedia from the ever diminishing emphasis on language, except in its illocutionary use.

147. "Formulate" implies a static one-to-one correspondence to a thought, a simplistic picture theory that need give way to a defining process in which inchoate ideas play off each other.

148. After all, there is in Wittgenstein's later aphorisms an unresolved

There is the satisfaction of getting things right evident in the first creative act, "and God saw that it was good." What was created measured up presumably to an inchoate idea. There is embedded in our thought an inescapable correspondence relationship common to both getting-it-right judgments and true statements. In the former, however, what the judgment corresponds to is seldom put into words, certainly not to the extent required by Tarski's formulation. That is a failure of articulation. Or, to push beyond the last lines of the *Tractatus,* how can we be fair to the vividness of this feeling of correspondence where articulation fails?

Toward a Unified Field Theory

We started with a bewildering array of conceptions of judgment. Can we now without procrustean measures fit them into one resting place? Some minor surgery is needed at the outset. We need to lop off the extremities of Kant's view of one function of judgment as the application of rules to exclude it from self-evident read-off applications such as the use of "chair." No decision, no fallibility, no process. For the same reason we must excise cases of mere assertion *qua* assertion as in Frege and Wittgenstein. These excisions are sanctioned by all but philosophical use. We are then left with the vital body of Kant's insight on rule application as it accounts for the vast area of everyday and professional judgments, including those by courts. We saw that Kant's other function of judgment, as one of arriving at the general from the particular, has wide application in the characterization and assessment of events. Indeed, it is fundamental to our use of language. But again, what is argued here is a narrower and tighter

---

ambivalence about language: we are its total captives, yet we must avoid its traps. In other words, avoid them by the appeal to right thinking, albeit only formulated in an alternative language. Even this hope for an active role for the thinker is denied by the passivity implicit in Heidegger's dictum: "It is language that thinks" (Tugendhat 1992, 107, translation mine).

conception of judgment, one that does not cover the whole cognitive field. Instead, this conception commensurate with usage sees the mark of judgment as grappling consciously with the particular case at hand which may involve moving both up and down in abstraction.

But there is another large domain of usage at the heart of Locke's conception of judgment as estimate, as a stand-in for knowledge. Locke's approach is structurally similar to Frege's as the conjoining of ideas, but one critical step back in definitiveness. We judge when we are not in a position to assert the truth with assurance. But what can a judgment on the distance of a tree have in common with the judgment of a court? Again we must be careful to cut away what are sometimes called perceptual judgments, that is seeing the tree. No decision, no fallibility, no process. But the estimate of its distance satisfies these three conditions, as does a judgment by a court. In each case we have a process through a decision to a belief that is a stand-in for knowledge, objective, prescriptive, but fallible.

These examples, drawn from the contrasting views of Kant and Locke, stand at the extremes of the wide range of cases turned up in the preceding pages. In this regard, beside sharing the three conditions discussed, all share to a greater or lesser degree considerations of importance and appropriateness in the process of reaching the decision. Clearly these elements are not as evident in estimating the distance of a tree as in determining right conduct in a social context. Yet we need remember how prominent they are in the derivative concept of "to take the measure of something," inherent in judgment. Finally, we have seen that the line between applying concepts and forming concepts is blurred, so that judgment plays a role in concept formation itself. A theory that sees weighting and fitting as central to all exercises of judgment can serve in the field to plot instances in the range and mark off other cognitive functions. Put in a way that would have found favor with Aristotle, exercises of judgment are just those deliberations in which determinations of importance and appropriateness are themselves central.

There remains the position that sees judgment as the endpoint of deliberation or thought. But there is nothing in this view, taken no farther, to distinguish judgment from belief, which Dewey held was the outcome of inquiry. While such a view acknowledges a prior deliberative process, there is no recognition of what is peculiar in such deliberation to the exercise of judgment to justify our distinct usage. The identification of judgment with single-strand belief tends to slip forward to *justified belief,* leading to a confusion of judgment and knowledge. This misses the distinction between judgment as fallible and complex, and knowledge as unqualified and simple. For knowledge, notwithstanding its necessary conditions, is (*pace* Dewey) unitary and static. Judgment isn't. Nothing hangs on the grammar. To judge, to exercise judgment, judgment as its result and as a derivative quality of mind, all bear the same hallmarks. Questions of judgment are just those that call for its exercise. At the end of the day we may come to believe that the breadth of the concept matches the complex mental process of getting things right.

Coda

In this essay I have made much of judgment because it cries out for treatment. I started out simply to understand its daily use and abuse witnessed on every side in professional life, in politics, and in the commercial world. I was puzzled that since Aristotle little had been written and even less incorporated into a comprehensive account of the exercise of judgment as an explanation of human success and achievement. I have attempted the beginnings of such an account to bring judgment in from the wings to center stage.

But the case for judgment should not be overstated. Intelligence in its traditional sense and imagination are just as critical, indeed primary. Judgment is no substitute for genius. Someone said genius is arriving at a destination without travelling there—but this is a travel book. While the concepts of intelligence and imagination may be difficult to pin down, they have proved workable and useful. The concept of judgment is equally so. Intelligence, imagination, and judgment compose a trinity to which much is owed. Judgment itself can be expanded as a matrix of a further trinity of process, decision, and belief, dependent on determinations of importance and appropriateness. The slight stream devoted to judgment needs to rejoin the main flow of inquiry.

No summary of what has been discussed is possible because what has been said is itself a catalogue of hints and conclusions linked to provoke exploration. There remains a tag-end. The emphasis on judgment may give the impression of tilting the balance toward relativism and subjectivity. The opposite is the intent and result. "Questions of judgment" have usually been thought of as subjective to distinguish them from knowledge thought of as objective. At the outset, the elements of importance and appropriateness, weight and fit seemed only to graze the periphery of cognition. But if we accept the reality of knowledge and accept the judgmental function as a necessary ingredient in all but its simplest forms, it follows that whatever line there is between objective and subjective should, once importance and appropriateness are let inside the tent, be drawn on the far side of the whole cognitive function and judgment given its due.[149] That so much reduces to questions of judgment does not enlarge the

---

149. A Kantian would say we must admit our capacity to recognize importance and appropriateness into the pantheon of Categories which guarantee the holistic reality of our known world. But the plausibility of any such built-in guarantee will depend on maintaining the previously discussed distinction between such recognitions and preferences. Perhaps in a roundabout way we have answered our initial question why Kant uses "judgment" to pose his question in the first *Critique*.

A variation of a Kantian account for the accord (Übereinstimmung) of fundamental judgments is to argue analogously from Noam Chomsky's deep grammar underlying all language to an expanded inborn structure that determines such judgments.

The third and purest play is indicated by the Fregean Platonist position sketched by Tyler Burge (1992). But because, as we have seen, no fast line can be drawn between sorts of judgment, the challenge to this position is whether it can be extended from the pristine intuitions of black-and-white logical truths (not judgments at all) to the wide, grey world of its everyday exercise.

sphere of the subjective. Rather, it brings us up against the rub that the application of the general and abstract imposes on us. If importance and appropriateness can't be uncoupled from knowledge, neither can the fields where judgment is traditionally seen to roam. Nor can objectivity be salvaged for cognition by relegating these outlying areas to subjectivity. Realists and cognitivists cannot hope to put daylight between themselves and these troubling notions. The upshot of a rejection of this schism is to see that we must enlist a rethought objectivity for an even wider and deeper role in cognition.

Our highest intellectual achievement is not simply formulating abstractions of great power, simplicity, and elegance, but tethering them convincingly to the particulars below. Unless a purely formal notion of truth is held sufficient,[150] truth lies with the meticulous application of theories and abstractions to particular events. Judgment is critical in that application; and the ideas thrown up by intelligence and imagination can only be put to use through it. The proof lies in the practice around us. Just as reality ultimately inheres in particular events, so does truth in statements about such events. We start as Platonists and end as Aristotelians. Though we are enmeshed in beliefs, the knots are tested one by one. It's this patch of snow that's white. It's this act that's right. It is the single decision, the single belief, the single act that counts epistemologically, socially, and morally.

---

150. Tarski's (1949, 52) semantic formulation accommodates particular statements and general statements equally well. What is left open is how to deal with mass terms (snow) and how far we can press the distinction between particular and general statements.

Bibliography

Achinstein, Peter, Maya Bar-Hillel, and A. Margalit. 1978–1981. "Discussion." *Mind* (January 1978, October 1979, January 1981).

Arendt, Hannah. 1977. "The Crisis in Culture." In *Between Past and Future*. Harmondsworth, UK: Penguin.

———. 1978. *Life of the Mind: Thinking, Willing*. New York: Harcourt, Brace, Jovanovich.

Argyris, Chris, and D. A. Schön. 1974. *Theory in Practice*. San Francisco: Josey-Bass Publishers.

———. 1978. *Organizational Learning: A Theory of Action Perspective*. Reading, Mass.: Addison-Wesley Publishing Co.

Aristotle. 1955. *Ethics [The Nicomachean Ethics]*, trans. J. A. K. Thomson. Harmondsworth, UK: Penguin Books.

Arrow, Kenneth J. 1951. *Social Choice and Individual Value*. New York: John Wylie.

Atiyah, P. S. 1981. *Promises, Morals and Law*. Oxford: Clarendon Press.

Audi, Robert. 1989. *Practical Reasoning*. London & New York: Routledge.

Austin, J. L. 1964. *Sense and Sensibilia*. London: Oxford University Press.

Ayer, A. J. 1980. *Hume*. London: Hill & Wang.

Baier, Kurt. 1958. *The Moral Point of View.* Ithaca, N.Y.: Cornell University Press.

Barraclough, C. 1960. "Scientific Method and the Work of the Historian." In Nagel, Suppes, and Tarski 1960.

Barry, Brian. 1965. *Political Argument.* London: Routledge and Kegan Paul.

Bell, David. 1987. "The Art of Judgement." *Mind* 96, no. 382 (April).

Bennett, Jonathan. 1974. *Kant's Dialectic.* Cambridge: Cambridge University Press.

Berlin, I. 1969. *Four Essays on Liberty.* Oxford: Oxford University Press.

———. 1980. *Against the Current.* New York: Viking.

Black, Max. 1954. *Problems of Analysis.* London: Routledge & Kegan Paul.

Boghossian, P. 1989. "Rule-following Considerations." *Mind* 98 (October).

Borradori, G. 1994. *The American Philosopher.* Chicago: University of Chicago Press.

Bowden, Margaret. 1977. *Artificial Intelligence and Natural Man.* New York: Basic Books.

Brooks, Cleanth. 1947. *The Well-Wrought Urn.* New York: Harcourt, Brace & World.

Broome, John. 1991. *Weighing Goods.* Oxford: Basil Blackwell.

Buchler, Justus. 1955. *The Nature of Judgement.* New York: Grosset & Dunlap.

Burge, Tyler. 1992. "Frege on Knowing the Third Realm." *Mind* (October).

Cairns, Alan C. 1988. *Constitution, Government and Society in Canada: Related Essays,* ed. D. E. Williams. Toronto, Ontario, Canada: McClelland and Stewart.

Carnap, Rudolf. 1949. "The Two Concepts of Probability." In *Readings and Philosophical Analysis,* ed. H. Feigl and W. Sellars. New York: Appleton-Century-Crofts.

———. 1960. "The Aim of Inductive Logic." In Nagel, Suppes, and Tarski 1960.

Carr, E. H. 1990. *What is History?* Harmondsworth, UK: Penguin.

Castellan, N. J., D. B. Pison, and G. R. Potts, eds. 1977. *Cognitive Theory,* vol. 2. Hillsdale, N.J.: Lawrence Erlbaum Associates.

Cavell, Marcia. 1993. *The Psychoanalytic Mind.* Cambridge, Mass.: Harvard University Press.

Cavell, Stanley. 1969. *Must We Mean What We Say?* New York: Charles Scribner's Sons.

———. 1990. *Conditions Handsome and Unhandsome.* Chicago & London: University of Chicago Press.

Chomsky, Noam. 1992. *Language and Problems of Knowledge.* Cambridge, Mass.: MIT Press.

Churchland, P. M. 1990. *Matter and Consciousness.* Cambridge, Mass.: MIT Press.

Cohen, Jonathan. 1977. *The Probable and the Provable.* Oxford: Clarendon Press.

Cohen, Marshall, ed. 1984. *Ronald Dworkin and Contemporary Jurisprudence.* London: Duckworth.

Cohen, Ted, and Paul Guyer, eds. 1982. *Essays on Kant's Aesthetics.* Chicago & London: University of Chicago Press.

Culler, Jonathan. 1989. *On Deconstruction.* Ithaca, N.Y.: Cornell University Press.

Currie, Gregory. 1993. "Interpretation and Objectivity." *Mind* 102 (July).

Davidson, Donald. 1980. *Essays on Actions and Events.* Oxford: Clarendon Press.

———. 1984. *Inquiries Into Truth and Interpretation.* Oxford: Clarendon Press.

———. 1986. *Knowing One's Mind.* Presidential address to the Pacific Division of the American Philosophical Assn. Berkeley: University of California.

Dennett, Daniel C. 1988. "When Philosophers Encounter Artificial Intelligence." In *The Artificial Intelligence Debate: False Starts Real Foundations,* ed. S. R. Graubard. Cambridge, Mass.: MIT Press.

Dennett, Daniel C. 1988. *The Intentional Stance.* Cambridge, Mass.: MIT Press.

Dewey, John. 1922. *Human Nature and Conduct.* New York: Henry Holt.

———. 1930. *The Quest for Certainty.* London: George Allen & Unwin.

———. 1982. *Logic the Theory of Inquiry.* New York: Irvington Publishers.

Dray, W. 1960. "The Historian's Problem of Selection." In Nagel, Suppes, and Tarski 1960.

Dummett, Michael. 1973. *Frege.* London: Duckworth.

———. 1978. *Truth and Other Enigmas.* Cambridge, Mass.: Harvard.

Dworkin, R. 1978. *Taking Rights Seriously.* London: Duckworth.

———. 1985. *A Matter of Principle.* Cambridge, Mass.: Harvard University Press.

———. 1986. *Law's Empire.* Cambridge, Mass.: Harvard University Press.

Elshtain, Jean Bethke. 1993. *Democracy on Trial.* Concord, Ontario, Canada: Anansi Press.

Elster, J. 1989. *Solomonic Judgments.* Cambridge: Cambridge University Press.

Emerson, Ralph Waldo. 1883. *Essays.* Boston: Houghton Mifflin.

Empson, William. 1953. *Seven Types of Ambiguity.* London: Chatto & Windus.

Feyerabend, Paul. 1978. *Against Method, Outline of an Anarchist's Theory of Knowledge.* London: Verso Edition.

Fish, Stanley. 1980. "How to Recognize a Poem When You See One." In *Is There a Text in This Class?* Cambridge, Mass.: Harvard University Press.

———. 1982. "Working on the Chain Gang: Interpretation in Law and Literature." *Texas Law Review* 60: 527.

Fodor, Jerry. 1978. "Propositional Attitudes." *Monist* 61 (4): 177.

Frege, Gottlob. 1966. *Logische Untersuchungen.* Göttingen: G. Petzig.

Fry, Roger. 1939. *Last Lectures.* Cambridge: Cambridge University Press.

Fukuyama, Francis. 1992. *The End of History and the Last Man.* New York: The Free Press/Macmillan.

Gadamer, Hans-Georg. 1976. *Philosophical Hermeneutics,* trans. and ed. David E. Linge. Berkeley: University of California Press.

———. 1987. "Hermeneutics as Practical Philosophy." In *After Philosophy, End or Transformation?* ed. K. Baynes, J. Bohman, and T. McCarthy. Cambridge, Mass: MIT Press.

———. 1992. *Truth and Method,* trans. Joel Weisheimer and Donald G. Marshall. New York: Crossroads.

Gardner, Howard. 1983. *Frames of Mind: The Theory of Multiple Intelligences.* New York: Basic Books.

Gauthier, David. 1963. *Practical Reasoning.* Oxford: Clarendon Press.

Gleick, James. 1987. *Chaos—Making A New Science.* New York: Penguin.

Graubard, S. R., ed. 1988. *The Artificial Intelligence Debate: False Starts, Real Foundations.* Cambridge, Mass.: MIT Press.

Haack, Susan. 1995. *Evidence and Inquiry.* Oxford: Blackwell.

Hare, R. M. 1952. *The Language of Morals.* Oxford: Clarendon.

Harman, Gilbert. 1977. *The Nature of Morality.* New York: Oxford University Press.

Hart, H. L. A. 1961. *The Concept of Law.* Oxford: Oxford University Press.

Hawking, Stephen. 1990. *A Brief History of Time.* New York: Bantam.

Herrnstein, R. J., and C. Murray. 1994. *The Bell Curve: Intelligence and Class Structure in American Life.* New York: Free Press.

Hofstadter, Douglas. 1980. *Gödel, Escher, Bach: An Eternal Golden Braid.* New York: Vintage Books.

Holyoak, Keith J., and Barbara A. Spellman. 1993. "Thinking." *Annual Review of Psychology.*

Hume, David. 1975. *A Treatise on Human Nature.* Oxford: Clarendon Press.

Hurley, S. L. 1989. *Natural Reasons.* Oxford: Oxford University Press.

Janis, I. L. 1972. *Victims of Groupthink.* Boston: Houghton Mifflin Company.

Jeffrey, R. C. 1983. *The Logic of Decision.* Chicago: University of Chicago Press.

Kant, I. 1957. *Critique of Judgment,* trans. J. C. Meredith. Oxford: Clarendon.

———. 1985. *Critique of Pure Reason,* trans. N. Kemp Smith. London: Macmillan.

Klagge, J. 1990. "Davidson's Trouble with Supervenience." *Synthese* 85.

Korner, Stephan, ed. 1974. *Practical Reason.* Oxford: Blackwell.

Kretschmer, Martin. 1993. Review of *A Progress of Sentiments* by Annette C. Baier (Cambridge, Mass.: Harvard, 1991), and *Hume's Theory of Moral Judgment* by Walter Brand (Dordrecht: Kluwer, 1992). *Mind* 102 (April).

Kripke, Saul. 1982. *Wittgenstein on Rules and Private Language.* Cambridge, Mass.: Harvard University Press.

Kuhn, T. S. 1970. *The Structure of Scientific Revolutions.* Chicago: University of Chicago Press.

Lehman, David. 1991. *Signs of the Times: Deconstruction and the Fall of Paul de Man.* New York: Poseidon Press.

Locke, John. 1964. *An Essay Concerning Human Understanding.* London: Dent, Everyman edition.

Lormond, E. 1990. "Framing the Frame Problem." *Synthese* 82.

Low-Beer, F. 1964. "The Concept of Neutralism." *American Political Science Review* 58.

———. 1968. "Carter's Logic." *Canadian Tax Journal,* no. 5.

———. 1989. "Dworkin's Empire and What Goes On in the Courtroom." *Queens Law Journal* 14, no. 2 (Winter).

Lycan, W. G. 1988. *Judgment and Justification.* Chapel Hill: University of North Carolina Press.

McDowell, John. 1994. *Mind and World.* Cambridge, Mass.: Harvard University Press.

McFetridge, I. G. 1975. "Propositions and Indirect Discourse." *Proceedings of the Aristotelian Society.*

Magee, Bryan, et al. 1978. *Men of Ideas.* London: British Broadcasting Corporation.

Matlin, Margaret. 1983. *Cognition.* New York: Holt, Rinehart & Winston.

Miller, Jonathan. 1983. *States of Mind.* New York: Pantheon Books.

Minsky, Marvin. 1985. *The Society of Mind.* New York: Simon & Schuster.

Montaigne. 1743. *Essays,* trans. C. Cochrane. London.

Murphy, John P. 1990. *Pragmatism from Peirce to Davidson.* San Francisco: Westview Press.

Nagel, E., P. Suppes, and A. Tarski, eds. 1960. *Logic, Methodology and Philosophy of Science.* Proceedings of the 1960 International Congress. Stanford, Calif.: Stanford University Press.

Nagel, Thomas. 1986. *The View from Nowhere.* London: Oxford University Press.

Nozick, Robert. 1981. *Philosophical Explanations.* Cambridge, Mass.: Harvard University Press.

———. 1993. *The Nature of Rationality.* Princeton, N.J.: Princeton University Press.

Oakeshott, Michael. 1962. *Rationalism in Politics.* New York: Methuen.

Parkinson, G. H. R. 1954. *Spinoza's Theory of Knowledge.* Oxford: Clarendon Press.

Penrose, Roger. 1994. *Shadows of the Mind.* Oxford: Oxford University Press.

Pettit, P. 1990. "The Reality of Rule Following." *Mind* 99 (January).

Pitcher, G., ed. 1964. *Truth.* Englewood-Cliffs, N.J.: Prentice Hall.

Pitz , G. F., and N. J. Sachs. 1984. "Judgment and Decision." *Annual Review of Psychology.*

Plato. 1982. In *The Collected Dialogues of Plato,* trans. M. Cornford. Princeton, N.J.: Princeton University Press.

Pugh, George E. 1977. *The Biological Origin of Human Values.* New York: Basic Books.

Putnam, Hilary. 1976. "What is Realism?" *Proceedings of the Aristotelian Society.*

——. 1988. "Much Ado About Not Very Much." In *The Artificial Intelligence Debate: False Starts, Real Foundations,* ed. S.R. Graubard. Cambridge, Mass.: MIT Press.

——. 1991. *Renewing Philosophy.* Cambridge, Mass.: Harvard University Press.

Quine, W. V. 1953. *From a Logical Point of View.* Cambridge, Mass: Harvard University Press.

——. 1960. *Word and Object.* Cambridge, Mass.: MIT Press.

——. 1981. *Theories and Things.* Cambridge, Mass.: Bellknap Press, Harvard University Press.

Rawls, J. 1972. *A Theory of Justice.* Oxford: Oxford University Press.

Raz, Joseph. 1978. *Practical Reasoning.* Oxford: Oxford University Press.

Rorty, R. 1979. *Philosophy and the Mirror of Nature.* Princeton, N.J.: Princeton University Press.

Rumfitt, Ian. 1993. "Content and Context: The Paratactic Theory Revisited and Revised." *Mind* 102 (July).

Russell, Bertrand. 1962. *An Inquiry into Meaning and Truth.* Harmondsworth, UK: Penguin.

Ryle, G. 1949. *The Concept of Mind.* New York: Barnes & Noble.

Sallis, John, ed. 1988. *Deconstruction and Philosophy: The Texts of Jacques Derrida.* Chicago & London: University of Chicago Press.

Schum, D. 1977. "The Behavioral Richness of Cascaded Inference Models." In *Cognitive Theory,* vol. 2, ed. N. J.

Castellan, D. B. Pisoni, and G. R. Potts. Hillsdale, N.J.: Lawrence Erlbaum Associates.

Schumpeter, J. A. 1950. *Capitalism, Socialism and Democracy.* New York: Harper.

Searle, John. 1983. *Intentionality.* Cambridge: Cambridge University Press.

———. 1985. *Speech Acts.* Cambridge: Cambridge University Press.

———. 1994. *The Rediscovery of the Mind.* Cambridge, Mass.: MIT Press.

Shephard, R., and P. Podgorny. 1978. "Cognitive Processes that Resemble Perceptual Processes." In *Handbook of Learning and Cognitive Processes,* vol. 5, ed. W. K. Estes. Hillsdale, N.J.: Lawrence Erlbaum Associates.

Smith, Lynn. 1987. "Heightened Objectivity." *The Advocate* (January).

Stalnaker, Robert C. 1984. *Inquiry.* Cambridge, Mass.: MIT Press.

Steinberger, Peter J. 1993. *The Concept of Political Judgment.* New York & Chicago: University of Chicago Press.

Steiner, George. 1975. *After Babel.* New York: Oxford University Press.

Sternberg, Robert. 1988. *The Triarchic Mind: A New Theory of Human Intelligence.* New York: Viking.

Sternberg, Robert, and Richard Wagoner, eds. 1986. *Practical Intelligence: Nature and Origins of Competence in the Everyday World.* Cambridge: Cambridge University Press.

Sukenick, Ronald. 1967. *Wallace Stevens: Musing the Obscure.* New York: New York University Press.

Tarski, A. 1949. "The Semantic Conception of Truth." In *Readings and Philosophical Analysis,* ed. H. Feigl and W. Sellars. New York: Appleton-Century-Crofts.

Taylor, Charles. 1991. *The Malaise of Modernity.* Concord, Ontario, Canada: Anansi.

Thalberg, I. 1972. *Enigmas of Agency.* London: George Allen & Unwin; New York: Humanities Press.

Thalberg, I. 1977. *Perception, Emotion and Action.* Oxford: Basil Blackwell.

Toulmin, Stephen. 1972. *Human Understanding,* vol. 1. Princeton, N.J.: Princeton University Press.

Tribe, Laurence H. 1992. "The 27th Amendment Joins the Constitution." *Wall Street Journal,* Wednesday, May 13.

Tugendhat, E. 1986. *Self-Consciousness and Self-Determination.* Cambridge, Mass., and London: MIT Press.

————. 1992. *Philosophische Aufsätze.* Frankfurt am Main: Suhrkamp.

Tversky, A., and D. Kahneman. 1981. "The Framing of Decisions and the Psychology of Choice." *Science* 211: 453–58.

Walders, Joseph, and Howard Gardner. 1986. "The Theory of Multiple Intelligences." In Sternberg and Wagoner 1986.

Walker, Ralph C. S. 1978. *Kant.* London: Routledge & Kegan Paul.

Wang, Hao. 1986. *Beyond Analytic Philosophy.* Cambridge, Mass.: MIT Press.

Wasserstrom, Richard A. 1961. *The Judicial Decision.* Stanford, Calif.: Stanford University Press.

Weiskrantz, L., ed. 1988. *Thought Without Language.* Oxford: Clarendon.

Whitehead, A. N. 1955. *The Concept of Nature.* Cambridge: Cambridge University Press.

Wiggins, David. 1975. "Deliberation and Practical Reason." *Proceedings of the Aristotelian Society.*

Wittgenstein, L. 1953. *Philosophical Investigations,* ed. and trans. G. E. Anscombe. Oxford: Basil Blackwell.

————. 1960. *Tractatus Logico-Philosophicus.* London: Routledge & Kegan Paul.

————. 1969. *On Certainty,* ed. G. E. M. Anscombe and G. H. von Wright. Oxford: Basil Blackwell.

————. 1974. *Letters to Bertrand Russell, 1912–1935,* ed. G. H. von Wright. Oxford: Basil Blackwell.

————. 1988. *Remarks on the Philosophy of Psychology,* vol. 1, ed. G. E. M. Anscombe and G. H. von Wright. Chicago: University of Chicago Press.

Wright, Crispin. 1992. *Truth and Objectivity.* Cambridge, Mass.: Harvard University Press.

———. 1993. *Realism, Meaning and Truth.* 2d ed. Oxford: Blackwell.

Name Index

213